finding naasicaa

letters of hope in an age of anxiety

finding naasicaa

letters of hope in an age of anxiety

charles ringma

REGENT COLLEGE PUBLISHING
Vancouver, British Columbia

Also by the same author:

Catch the Wind: A Precursor to the Emergent Church
Life in Full Stride: Faith-Stretching Reflections for
Christians in the Real World
Whispers from the Edge of Eternity: Reflections on Life and
Faith in a Precarious World

Cry Freedom with Voices From the Third World
Dare to Journey with Henri Nouwen
Let My People Go with Martin Luther King, Jr.
Resist the Powers with Jacques Ellul
Seek the Silences with Thomas Merton
Seize the Day with Dietrich Bonhoeffer
The Seeking Heart: A Journey with Henri Nouwen
Wash the Feet of the World with Mother Teresa

For

a new generation:
bearers of hope for a newer tomorrow;

for a past generation of parents:
whose spiritual faith fractured with the collapse of
Christendom;

and for an older generation of grandparents:
whose life is marked by anxious prayer.

Published 2006 by Regent College Publishing
in association with Piquant Agency

Revised edition, 2007

5800 University Boulevard, Vancouver, BC V6T 2E4 Canada
Web: www.regentpublishing.com
E-mail: info@regentpublishing.com

Regent College Publishing is an imprint of the Regent Bookstore <www.regentbookstore.com>. Views expressed in works published by Regent College Publishing are those of the author and do not necessarily represent the official position of Regent College <www.regent-college.edu>.

Library and Archives Canada Cataloguing in Publication

Ringma, Charles
Finding Naasicaa : letters of hope in an age of anxiety / Charles Ringma.

Includes bibliographical references and index.
ISBN 1-57383-358-4

1. Christian life. 2. Faith. 3. Ringma, Charles Correspondence.
I. Title.

BV4501.3.R547 2006   248.4   C2005-902624-3

contents

preface

I have written this book for my oldest grandchild, Naasicaa. She is nineteen years of age and is presently attending university.

My purpose for writing is, on the one hand, simple enough. I wanted to share with her something of the Christian story and my own joyful and at times difficult journey of faith. In doing this, I have the hope that this storytelling might also be helpful to others, particularly those who know snippets of the Christian faith, but have doubts about its claims and relevance.

But of course, there are always more complex reasons for writing. We are never subject to singular motivations. We usually do things for many reasons and some of these may remain hidden even to ourselves.

One of these more complex reasons is that the opportunity to restate the Christian story and to reflect on my own journey of faith has provided me with the opportunity for renewal and recovery. What I mean by this is that storytelling is a way of deepening the story for oneself.

Another factor is that I feel that I owe Naasicaa and others like her something. What that something is, is rather difficult to bring into words. Perhaps one way of getting close is to acknowledge that to believe and to live the Christian story in our present culture is much more difficult than when I was young. In my youth the Christian story was generally held in much higher regard. Today there is much doubt, even cynicism.

This of course does not mean that I see myself in a better position and that I can talk with confidence while others doubt. I have no such superior attitude. In fact, these very things raise a serious problem, namely, that my faith shaped in a different time may not be able to appreciate fully or relate to the difficulties and issues of our present time. I guess that only you, the reader, will be able to determine the extent to which my storytelling has been relevant and helpful.

While this book has in view a wider audience, it is also about the celebration of family, intergenerational links and the passing on of stories and values. So I wish to honour my children and grandchildren. I appreciate their individuality and creativity and their equally strong sense of mutual love and care.

The reader will note that the personal pronouns in relation to God are in inverted commas: 'He'. This is a way of indicating that God is Spirit and not a male figure as the use of He might otherwise indicate. In other words, God is beyond gender.

I especially wish to thank my daughter, Marina Ringma-McLaren for her enthusiastic assistance and for doing the work in completing the typescript, and Robert Hand for his editorial work and creativity in turning a manuscript into a book. A final thanks goes to Karen Hollenbeck-Wuest, whose editorial skills have made this book more readable.

Charles Ringma
Brisbane, Manila, Vancouver, Yangon
2005

an opening word for naasicaa

letter one

You will remember the 'Easter house', Naasicaa. For a number of years when Rita and I returned to Australia from the Philippines for a holiday we would all gather as an extended family at this beach house on Queensland's Sunshine Coast. It was always during the Easter period.

We still all talk about the 'Easter house'. Not only did we have a fun time there, but there was also the snake drama, among other memorable events, to add texture to our story telling.

The 'Easter house' has become part of the family folk lore. And in the telling and re-telling we almost relive the fun times and the drama.

We all carry many stories within us. Some we tell often. Others are barely mentioned. And sometimes the most important stories are never told because there doesn't seem to be an appropriate setting in which to tell them.

3

So in the form of a series of letters, I want to share with you some of the stories of life's meaning and purpose and matters of faith and spirituality.

The Christian story is a big story. It has its roots in the fascinating pages of the Old Testament. And it continues in the burst of activity around the person of Jesus Christ, which led to the formation of the early Christian communities and has continued up to the present. This story is thus thousands of years long. And obviously, this whole story cannot be told here. So I will have to highlight certain aspects of that story.

It is important for you to know that we usually make a distinction between the initial telling of the story as that has been recorded in the pages of the Bible and the way in which the story has unfolded in the history of the church over the past two thousand years. What I mean by this is that the recorded story has the priority over the way in which the church throughout its long history has sought to understand and live that story. Put differently, the Bible has priority over church tradition. This means that the story of the Bible can correct our story.

But in many ways, while basically correct, this distinction has many problems associated with it, and we will have to return to this issue as we go along. One difficulty is that we cannot understand an old story without taking our present issues, culture and history with us.[1] I realize that this rather bald statement may be difficult for you to grasp but hopefully this will become clearer as we go along.

In telling any story there are many ways to tell it and many forms of expression. It could be told as drama. But I am sharing the story in the form of a series of conversations that I have written in letter form. This is not quite as exciting as drama but I hope you will bear with my lack of creativity. I enjoy letter writing so I will make use of what I do best.

This of course is not to suggest that the Christian story and something of my experience of it are downright dull and boring.

You are probably well aware of the fact that we always seem to slant a story in a particular way. Put differently, depending on who we are talking to we tend to tell the story differently. This is in itself good, for it has to do not only with our sensitivity to the one to whom we are talking, but also our creativity. But there are problems with this as well. We may exaggerate the story. We may tell the good bits and leave the bad bits out. I have to be careful at this point in my storytelling. I must not make the Christian story and my participation in that story easier or nicer than it is. I don't want to fall into propaganda.

The main point that I want to get to in this first letter is to ask whether the story is worth telling. Is it one that we could simply ignore? It is obvious that I think the answer is, 'No, we can't ignore this story', otherwise I would not be writing to you. But let me give you several reasons why. The first is that Christianity is an important part of two thousand years of history. Western thinking, art, music and the general culture have all been influenced by Christianity. This is now true of other parts of the world as well. Secondly, the Christian story is worth thinking about because it provides insights into so much of what life is all about: the beginning of the world, the nature of human beings, the shape of the social order and the future that awaits us. It talks about love, suffering, death and hope. These and many other issues are matters that we all grapple with.

So where do we start with this big story? We could trace the story chronologically, starting with Genesis and following through to the book of Revelation, or we could move from early Christianity to the contemporary church. But I would like to tell the story differently. I think that talking about major *themes* would be a better way to go. I can then weave together scripture, church history, some of my own experience and then connect it to the contemporary world.

You know that each year I spend my time in Canada, Australia and Asia. My conversations with you are written in different parts of the world. Some of the flavour of these different settings will come through in what I write, and I think this is appropriate. The Christian story is no longer the story of the West. It is a world story.[2] In fact, it has always been that way, although for a long time it was predominantly a Western story.

The other important development is that many Western nations have become multi-cultural and many people travel and experience other parts of the globe. This has influenced the way we see and understand things. We are very aware of diversity, plurality and difference. This has implications for the way in which we understand the Christian story, particularly because Christianity is presently weak in the First World, but alive and virile in the Third World. Maybe others now know the Christian story better than we do. This calls for a new humility on our part and willingness to listen to others.

But this probably is enough of an introduction. (In fact, I sometimes wonder why we succumb to this literary device. Does an introduction sort of set the reader up?) Why not get to the story proper! It is in the story itself that the power lies. And the wonder of stories, particularly the big stories of humanity and of our world, is that they allow us to interface the small story of our lives with their grand themes. In this, we ourselves are enriched and become more fully human.

the world without and within

letter two

You may be a little surprised that I want to start here. You probably expected that I would begin to talk about the importance of faith or the necessity of prayer, or that I should begin to talk about God and everything else would flow from that starting point. After all, religion usually has to do with belief in a Deity and participating in the religious practices that flow from that belief.

But this is not where I wish to start. However, this does not mean that I do not think that God is centrally important and that faith can be relegated to the sidelines. Rather, I want to start, Naasicaa, with where you are. I want to talk about life, the kind of world in which we live and the way in which the world shapes us.

This last idea, the world within, is particularly important for us to think about. The world, and here I mean both nature and the social world (the world of cities, industries, institutions, culture), is not simply a world that lies outside of us. Of course it is out there, but it is also

7

within us in the sense that we are shaped by its institutions and values through the process of socialization. One of the reasons why I need to talk about this is that we are really not as free as we think we are. We think that we make a whole range of decisions, but often our choices are very much influenced by our family background, schooling and the way in which the general culture has influenced us. So this is an important issue that I wish to discuss and will return to in subsequent letters.

the world of nature

I am writing this letter in the home that I share with your aunt and uncle in Brisbane, Australia. It's a typical Queensland winter day. The temperature is 24 degrees. The sky is brilliant blue. The sun filtering through the palm trees in the backyard is doing a dance of light and shadow on my writing desk. I can hear the screech of rainbow lorikeets and the more melodious call of the butcher bird. As you know our backyard runs into bushland and then into parkland. One would hardly know that I am living in a big city. Nature is all around us. We see possums and bandicoots and ticks bite us from time to time reminding us that there is a snake in every paradise.

Like you, I love nature. The bleached beaches of Fraser Island, the lush subtropical rainforests of the Lamington Plateau, the stark Canadian Rockies and the exotic beauty of the island of Mindoro in the Philippines—these are only some of the beautiful places that I have experienced. And you, of course, love the beautiful Blue Mountains west of Sydney, where you spent some of your childhood.

I see the world of nature as a most wonderful gift from the Creator. It is a gift that sustains us and the billions of others who inhabit this planet. The natural world not only gives us food and water, but also all the resources we need to build our societies and to create our cultures.

While I do not believe that we should worship nature, I do believe that we need to appreciate it much more than we have done in the past. Previous attitudes towards nature took it for granted, believed it was inexhaustible in terms of resources and riches and as a result nature was exploited.

Sadly, the Christianity of the past number of centuries uncritically contributed to these faulty ideas. The Genesis story in the Bible was read in such a way that humanity was seen as having dominion over the natural world and this meant exploitation rather than care and stewardship. I think this was a misreading of the story. Care for the world rather than exploitation is central to the biblical message.

We now know better that we cannot keep on taking. All things need care and renewal. So does nature. And it has been a good development that we have become much more environmentally sensitive. Sadly, this has come belatedly, after so much environmental damage has already been done. And in many places this wanton madness continues.

Since you are an astute reader, you will have noticed that this brief discussion has already moved from the world of nature as such to what *we* do with nature. And this is precisely the issue with which we repeatedly have to grapple. Yes, there are wilderness areas and other locations where nature exists in its pristine beauty, but so much of the globe is an environment shaped by human hands. We have turned nature into landscape, and we have done that for very good reasons. Moving from hunter-gatherer communities to agricultural, to industrial and now post-industrial communities, we use the world of nature to sustain life and build our societies. That we have done this with some faulty ideas should not surprise us.

You and I both know that much more could and should be said about the world of nature. Nature is not a compliant 'mistress'. It does not yield its secrets easily. And when scorned nature has a way of retaliating. Many natural disasters are 'man'-made, and nature can be 'violent'. Having lived in the Philippines I do know something firsthand of the power of typhoons and earthquakes.

For a long time Christian theologians talked about God providing humanity with 'two books': the Bible and the book of nature. Some theologians believed that the book of nature would eventually lead us to want to understand the Bible. Nature, it was claimed, tells us something about the power and magnificence of God, while the Bible tells us about the person of God and 'his' involvement with humanity. I am not so sure about these neat ideas. It is more likely the other way round: knowing God as the redeemer helps us to appreciate God as the creator.

the social world

I don't know about you, but one of the things that has always impressed me is human ingenuity, creativity and diversity. The social world is like a kaleidoscope of contours and colours.

The social world often appears as a rock solid given. The language we speak, the way we structure family, the institutions we create, the way we produce things and do business and the political realities that govern our world all seem so permanent, even though they have to adapt to changing circumstances. While the world of a millennia or even centuries ago changed very slowly, that is not so now. In fact the opposite is the case. Our urban environment, institutions and values are all caught up in rapid change. Therefore I think we need to acknowledge that *uncertainty* is very much a part of our contemporary consciousness. This is surprising in light of the fact that we tend to regard our 'primitive' forebears as living in a world of uncertainty in the face of the forces of nature, while we claim that we have made the world secure through the power of science and technology. This security is really a myth. The very social and economic world that we have created now frequently threatens us.

You will not have failed to notice, Naasicaa, how quickly my discussion about the social world has moved to talking about some of its difficulties. This is not good, for we cannot live only problem-centred lives; we should also celebrate. We cannot only look at the world with critical eyes; we also need eyes of wonderment and appreciation.

So let me start with wonderment, and then return to the matter of critique. What particularly amazes me is the way in which we have been able to respond to different physical environments in order to create a diversity of societies and cultures. It seems that the human impulse is towards creative externalization, though this does not mean that we are not also creatures of tradition and continuity. We not only adopt what is given, but we also adapt. We not only receive what is given, but we also transform. We not only live with what we have, but we also create the new.

I believe that human creativity is a great gift and it is amazing how we have been able to utilise this creativity to build the kind of societies we have today. So in many ways you are blessed, Naasicaa: to grow up in the beautiful city of Sydney, to have parents and grandparents who love and respect you, to have the opportunity for good schooling, health care and lots of recreation in the land of surfing beaches. People around us serve us well and there is every reason to celebrate so much that is good. What is troublesome, however, is that those of us who live in the Western world are generally *not* thankful. We don't appreciate what we have. We want more. And this wanting more is the worrisome driving force in our culture. Contemporary capitalism functions by fanning an insatiable consumerism. We are told that our very happiness depends on our having the latest consumer product. As a consequence, we are not a culture that appreciates what we have; we are a culture of *complaint.*

You are probably smiling now and thinking that it doesn't take your grandfather too long before he gets back to the problems of our society. You are right, for while I do seek to celebrate all that is good in our culture, I do have some grave concerns. In summary, I am concerned about some of our core societal values and equally concerned about the growing gap between rich and poor countries and the gap between 'the haves' and 'the have-nots' in our own society.

But let me first back up a little bit. While the social world is the movement of tradition, it is also a world that we are making and shaping. And while the 'we' includes all of us, it particularly includes the elite and the culture bearers in our society. Put differently, those with power and influence are the ones who are shaping our world. While I am quite sure that many of those in power seek to shape our world for the common good, I am equally sure that others seek to shape the world in such a way that it primarily *benefits them.* As a consequence, I believe that real exploitation occurs in our world, that we are fed propaganda and that we are being manipulated by powerful interests and forces.

I wonder whether this makes me some sort of 'radical' in your eyes or maybe even a 'communist ideologue'. I am actually neither, but I am critical of aspects of our society. And I believe you are as well. In fact, many of your peers are questioning some of the previous certainties of modernity, including scientism and rationalism and the impact this has had on the political and economic processes of our time.

Let me briefly explain how my more critical stance came about. It certainly did not come from my family upbringing or my participation in the life of the church. My family was very conservative and the Reformed Church of which I was a part was more isolationist than socially engaging. I later learned that this should not have been the case. The Reformed tradition is fundamentally reformational and is a world-formative Christian movement.[1] In other words, it believes that Christians are in the world to change the world in the light of the Kingdom of God. But particular churches in particular points of history do not always live up to their own heritage. The Dutch Reformed Church in the former apartheid South Africa is a good example of this failure.

My more critical and radical orientation came from three interrelated sources. The first was through reading and re-reading the gospels in the New Testament. The message of Jesus with its emphasis on reconciliation, love, peace and care for the poor, is so different than what normally occurs in our world. Secondly, my work in urban mission made me aware of the gross injustice that occurs at street level. Not only are the poor neglected, but some the worst drug pushers were the police themselves. And finally, living in a Third World country for many years made me aware of questionable Western economic values and the nature of structural evil.

A critical approach to society need not be negative in orientation. It can be fundamentally positive, for it seeks to penetrate the rhetoric and propaganda that is constantly fed to us. We are told that individuals, companies and governments do things that will benefit us. But so frequently things are done that benefit them. Drug companies suppress information about harmful side-effects, multi-nationals hide their exploitative work practices, and governments give us information that will enhance their election prospects. We certainly cannot live gullible lives in our kind of world.

So let me come back then, to some of my central concerns. Contemporary Western values promote individualism, consumerism and self-preoccupation. We are taught to struggle by ourselves when the very nature of social life has to do with community and partnership. We are encouraged to desire things when happiness lies in relationships and inner values. And we think that the more we focus on and live for ourselves the happier we will be. This is not true. Emotional well-being includes being others-concerned and not simply self-preoccupied.

I am aware that you may simply respond with the suggestion that we either should not worry too much about these things or that we can't do much about these matters anyway. But we can't put our head in the sand and we can't be neutral. In fact, if we don't think about these things and do something about them, we simply contribute to the way the world is. Inaction is being for the status quo. To put that differently, we simply end up adding to the injustice and dysfunctionality of our world.

the world within

If you have followed the drift of my thinking so far, you will have realized that I am arguing for both an appreciation of our world and a critique of it. In more expensive language I am talking about a hermeneutics of affirmation that appreciates the value of tradition and a hermeneutics of suspicion[2] which questions much of the way things are.

But I am also suggesting something more. We cannot only think critically about our world; we also need to get our hands dirty. In other words, our critique and concern must lead to costly engagement. Here Karl Marx is suggestive with his famous dictum: the philosophers have tried to explain the world, but we must seek to change it.

Not only is this easier said than done, but we are no longer so sure in what direction we need to work for change. We certainly don't want to go in a state communist direction. That has been totally discredited. But capitalism isn't all that wonderful either. It has given us plenty of material goods but happiness escapes us and our social fabric is seriously torn. These are deep questions, and therefore we need to talk about the world within.

We often have the idea that the world within is our private inner world: it's the place where we hold our stories, memories, hopes and fears. The inner world is the world of our secrets, the place where we are safe. But, sadly, it is not so simple. Our inner world is not simply of our own making; it is also the internalization of the things around us. Or, to put that differently, our landscape becomes a part of our soulscape.

What this means is that through family, education and the institutions of our society, we imbibe a language, a whole set of values and particular ways of thinking. We are profoundly shaped by the world around us and that is one of the reasons why it is so difficult to see our world differently and critically. Peter Berger and Thomas Luckmann speak about the way in which we creative human beings 'externalize' ourselves through the creation of communities, artifacts and culture. Over time these become objectified; that is, they take on solidity and permanency. As such, they become internalized, and we begin to think that this is the way these things are: this is the way the world is, and maybe even needs to be. And so we accept our world, and don't even think about the need to change it.[3] Thinking about change often only occurs when we are in some sort of pain because things no longer 'work'.

So what I am suggesting to you, Naasicaa, is that the world without is also very much the world within. To a large extent this is good because socialization leads to social cohesion. But what is not so helpful is that we internalize not only what is good in our world, but also its pain, dysfunctionality and propaganda.

The 'stuff' we see on the mega-screen of world history is also the 'stuff' that is within us on a small scale. The greed, injustice and irrationality that we see around us are also, in some small way, within us. And that is a big worry. This means that the world within is not a peaceful world. And while we don't need to agree with every interpretation of Sigmund Freud regarding our inner world, he is right in pointing out that it is not a harmonious world. It is one of conflict, just as our outer world is such a world as well.

None of this seeks to deny the good, the beauty and the creativity that lie within us. Music, art, literature, architecture, culture, technology and so much more of human achievement reflects this ability to do good and to make beautiful. It reflects the power of the human spirit not to succumb but to overcome. It shows our ability to wrestle with our problems and difficulties and to work towards solutions.

This inner world requires a lot of care. It cannot be neglected. We cannot focus only on outward activity and forget about our inner person. We cannot be concerned only about building our cities and our economy and leave the heart unattended. If we do, we will not only become lopsided, but we will begin to suffer.

Maybe this is all old hat to you, or maybe you think that we can't really think about the world in this way because it is far too sombre. But you will let me know, won't you?

When I started writing, I constantly heard the shrieks of the rainbow lorikeets. They are gone now. I had placed birdseed and water for them in a tray on our back deck, but they made too much mess. Your grandmother asked me to move the birdfeed, but now the lorikeets have gone. Maybe you can't have beauty without having shit. Possibly, this letter has been somewhat about this.

life's meaning and uncertainty

letter three

I have been revising this letter to you since I returned to Canada. It's good to be back in our small basement apartment in East Vancouver. We live just off Commercial Drive and the neighbourhood teems with people from different cultures, although Italians, Asians and Latinos predominate. Sometimes, I am the only Caucasian on the bus that runs along the Drive.

Rita and I deliberately moved into this area even though this takes me far away from my work at Regent College on the University of British Columbia campus, which is on the other side of the city. Our move here was carefully thought through and has everything to do with some of the values we hold. I guess it has a lot to do with our life's meaning. But more of that later.

I have been revising this letter because it is not easy to write about life's meaning. It may be easier to write about life's uncertainties, which we all experience to greater or lesser degrees. But to deal with life's meaning invites us into the amazing diversity of life's experiences and into the recognition that different people make very different sense of life. What we can say is that where one lives and the culture one is a part of do have a lot to do with the meaning one makes of life in a broad sense, although here also we see great diversity. One can be an educated middle-class Caucasian Canadian and believe in primal religion, or one can be a First Nations person and be a dedicated Christian. These differing belief systems obviously impact the meaning these two individuals make of life.

meaning-making creatures

I think that a good place to start this reflection is to recognize that we are meaning-making creatures. We attempt to make sense of life. Or to put that only slightly differently, we spend a lot of time trying to understand others, our world and ourselves. In fact, Martin Heidegger goes so far as to suggest that our very being has to do with seeking to understand all that can be understood. Hence the ceaseless quest for knowledge.[1]

I broadly suggested in my earlier letter to you that there is some connection between understanding ourselves, others and our world. To seek to understand ourselves in isolation does not make a lot of sense. We best understand ourselves in relationship to others and the wider world of which we are a part. Thus our environment and our culture shape our self-understanding.

It is one thing to know this intellectually, but it's another thing altogether for this to be brought home when one transfers into a different socio-cultural setting. I never realized, for example, how middle-class my values were until I began to work among the urban poor in Australia. And I never realized how Western I was in my values, ideas and ways of thinking until I lived in Asia. What all of this means is that we don't make sense of our lives by ourselves; rather, we inherit our society and our place in it uncritically, without thinking about it.

But having said all of this, it is nevertheless true that you and I have to make our *own* sense of the world. And this is difficult. We soon realize that we can't even make sense of ourselves. We are complex in our feelings and motivations and we often sense that we are a mystery even to ourselves. And as for making sense of our world, that is even more daunting. The world is bewildering in its diversity. And there is so much specialized knowledge out there that many lifetimes would not be enough to even begin to read it all, let alone understand it. The consequence of this is that we are becoming more and more specialized in narrow areas of interest and are losing a grasp of the wider picture and the interconnectedness of life.

I think it is important to note that the journey toward making our own meaning of life is a bit of a lonely journey. It takes some courage, for we have to ask some difficult questions and we have to be willing to come to different opinions than those held by people around us, particularly the significant others in our lives.

I remember well when as a teenager I began to question whether I wanted to live the kind of life my parents were living. As migrants to Australia from The Netherlands their over-riding preoccupation in the new country seemed to be to build the good life—a life of material prosperity and well being. And I remember saying 'no' to my father's invitation to become a part of his business. Looking back over my life I can see that I have had to say 'no' often in many different settings and circumstances as I have attempted to live out my own sense of meaning and purpose. We don't make important decisions about what we believe and how we want to live only once. We have to do this again and again, so the idea that we are on a *journey* is a good metaphor.

The other thing that I should point out is that our quest in understanding life's meaning involves some pain. You have probably experienced this already, Naasicaa. When we hold something as being important and a friend of ours does not, then in time that may rupture the relationship. I disagreed with some of the teachings of the church of which I was a part in my younger days and consequently had to leave. This cost me quite a number of friendships.

So discovering life's meaning and purpose, while at times exhilarating, is also fraught with difficulties. And maybe that very both/and experience is central to the way we live life.

accepting limitation

Since we cannot read, experience and know everything, it becomes rather obvious that our understanding of life's meaning can never be exhaustive or comprehensive. It usually does not take us too long in life's journey to realize this.

This raises an interesting question: If we can't know everything, how can we be sure that we can know life's meaning? This is related to the idea that we can't understand the part unless we understand the whole.

There are various ways of responding to this fascinating issue. One way is simply to disconnect the idea of knowing everything and knowing life's meaning by stating that since I need to discover *my* meaning of life, I don't need to know everything. Another way is to acknowledge that I don't need to have exhaustive knowledge in order to really know something. I can truly love someone and yet not have exhaustive knowledge of that person.

But another way to proceed is to make sense of life by embracing a 'meta-narrative', a story that is big enough to deal with life and death, the individual and society, the past and the future. What I am suggesting here is that most of us don't simply create our own meaning of life but use existing religious or philosophical systems to help us make sense of life. We don't try to make sense of life simply *by* ourselves. This of course is not to deny that we do have to make sense of life *for* ourselves. What I am proposing here is that we don't start with a clean slate and start from the beginning and do it all by ourselves. This is not possible anyway. Heidegger speaks about our being 'thrown into the world'. What he means by that is that we are all socialized into a particular world of language, culture and values which shape us much more formatively than we realize. So in the West, whether we realize it or not, we are shaped by ancient Greek thought and by the Judeo-Christian tradition, by the Renaissance and the Reformation, by the Enlightenment and by Romanticism, by scientism and mysticism.

You may feel a little overwhelmed by my reference to these major formative movements of thought because you may have not yet had the opportunity to study them all. And that is okay for the moment. We will pick up on some of these matters later.

Even as I write this I can see your wrinkled brow, your flashing eyes and your reluctance. Talking about meta-narratives is possibly most 'uncool'. And I am not surprised if you would point out to me that many people in the Western world do not embrace some major philosophical or religious system, and many of these major systems have been discredited anyway.[2]

These are fair comments to make. In our contemporary culture there is great skepticism about the meta-narratives or the major ideologies of the past. State communism and the Christianity of the colonial period have been largely discredited. Much of the older views of science, with their underlying ideas of objectivity, control, progress and manipulation, also have been seriously questioned. This questioning is good. However, it is important to point out that one of the problems with meta-narratives is that over time the basic story gets embellished and often becomes distorted. Stalin's state communism was a far cry from the writings of Karl Marx and centuries of Christianity in the Middle Ages were a far cry from the gospel message of Jesus.

While many people may not have formally adopted a particular philosophical or religious system, even those who have no formal position nevertheless hold an informal perspective that is philosophically explainable. For example, a person may claim, 'I don't believe in anything and life has no meaning'. This comes close to the position of nihilism. But it will not be lost on you that this person *does* have a belief, namely, that nothing is worth believing.

So by way of basic recapitulation, I am simply pointing out that while we have to make meaning of life for ourselves, we usually adopt or adapt major ideas that are available to us. That is the only point that I wish to make now. I will later discuss how we can know whether the ideas that we embrace are good and beneficial. This is a huge concern, for history teaches us that people have accepted ideas that are harmful and destructive. We only need to think of the impact of Fascism in Germany, and in earlier days, notions of white superiority in the displacement of Aborigines in the settlement of what later became the nation of Australia.

purpose and paradox

I suppose it is true that there are people who sort of meander through life and never think too much about anything. As long as their basic needs are met, they seem to be happy enough. There are also millions of people who live in dire poverty, oppression and marginalization, whose most basic impulse is to survive and to work for the betterment of the next generation. Both groups have purpose: the one is not to be too concerned about anything, the other is survival and improvement.

In making sense of life we do need to talk about how we see life's purpose. While at school we have to begin thinking about what work we want to do. And while we may be influenced by very pragmatic reasons, such as, 'I want to work in the hospitality industry because that is where the jobs are', or, 'I want to become a lawyer because that is a high status and well paying career', what we wish to do also involves how we see our purpose in life.

So what is life's purpose? Here we need to be careful that we don't become reductionistic, making statements such as, 'My purpose in life is to be married', or 'to be famous' or 'to be rich', or to be a 'musician' or 'a missionary'. It seems to me that while some of these statements may give one's life a particular contour and direction, life's purpose is to be seen as being much broader and more comprehensive.

What I mean by this is that I am more than simply my career. And my purpose in life besides being a good lawyer may also be to be a caring wife and mother and to work voluntarily for marginalized youth. But even describing life's purpose in these terms is grossly inadequate. All of this is still too pragmatically focused. We can make more fundamental statements such as 'my purpose in life is to use my gifts for my loved ones and others' or 'my purpose in life is to love' or 'my purpose is to glorify God and serve others'. And whether we are a motor mechanic, farmer, professor, priest, or family and home caregiver, all or some of these more fundamental values can come to expression.

It is appropriate, I think, to ask at this point how this sense of purpose comes to us. This is difficult to answer, for it invites us into life's amazing diversity. For some a sense of purpose may come very early in life. We only need think of the young Mozart. Or the equally young Dietrich Bonhoeffer springs to mind who, at a very early age, knew he was to become a theologian.[3] But for most of us, life's purpose is a gradually unfolding reality. We feel our way *into* life. We make choices and modify them. Through our experiences of pleasure and pain we come to see what is worth living for.

I am not all that sure that we can say that we were born for a particular purpose, if we mean that a particular purpose is predetermined for us. I don't think that this is so, even in a religious sense. Some of the key people around Jesus were fishermen. They later became apostles. (An exception to this seems to be John the Baptist who, from birth, was marked for a prophetic role. And, of course, this was also true of Jesus himself.)

But for most of us our sense of purpose and vocation unfolds. And frequently, it is simply a surprise. I entered the printing and publishing industry as a young man and loved this kind of work with all its creativity. I had no idea that I would end up being a specialized urban youth worker and later a theological educator.

So it's important to touch on the paradoxical dimensions around these issues. One is the basic observation that it is often not the formal situations of life that provide us with the opportunities to express who we are, our values and how we want to benefit and bless others. It is often what we do informally, along the way and incidentally, that provides us with the opportunity to realize what we most fully seek to be on about. The other is that sometimes we just 'fall into' doing something, and it is only later, as we look back, that we see some sort of pattern. Others again are drawn into life's purpose through circumstances and events that almost 'overtake' them. This was true of Dr. Martin Luther King, Jr., who was drawn into the civil rights struggle and was thrown into national prominence.[4]

a personal reflection

I know you probably want to ask me what I think about life's meaning and purpose. In one sense this whole book is an attempt to answer this important question, but I will make some initial responses to this. Bear with me if this is not as comprehensive or as specific as you may have wished.

I want to begin by emphasizing that understanding life's purpose has very much to do with seeing life as a most precious gift. Life itself, and so much more, is given to us. By the 'so much more', I am referring to family, friends, education, resources and the list goes on and on. And who we are, with our physicality, talents, personality and intellectual resources, is sheer giftedness. This, of course, is not to deny that we don't contribute to this by the life choices we make and the kind of life-style we live. We are not set in cement so that everything about us is a pre-given. But we cannot wholly remake ourselves either. We have to learn to accept our physicality and giftedness and live *into* what we have and are, rather than *against* who we are. Sadly, some people never learn the gentle art of self-acceptance and continuously do violence to themselves by trying to be something other than who they are.

Let me further unpack some of the things I am saying here. The first is that the most basic movement of life is not giving, but receiving. Life is not first of all demand, but a blessing. It is not first of all what we *do* with all our energy and talents, but who we *are*. Secondly, I believe that life can only be lived meaningfully and purposefully if it is lived with gratitude. If we live life with resentment and demand then the very fabric of our lives will become distorted. And finally, much of life has to do with learning the difficult art of acceptance. We have to accept the way we look, the intellectual and artistic gifts we have been given, our biological health and the way we are oriented.

I further believe that we can't squeeze life's meaning out of life in a similar way to juicing an orange. Life unfolds. It is appropriate to speak of one's life's 'cycle', or to put that differently, to speak of life's major transition points in the journey from childhood to adulthood and old age. And each of these phases has its own contribution to make in terms of our psycho-social development and our growth in understanding life's purpose and mystery. I have the writings of Erik Erikson in view here.[5]

It seems to me that we need to live life with a great capacity for openness. This in no way denies the importance to plan and to make choices about relationships, place, work and life-style. But much comes to us not as a result of our planning and doing, but by way of surprise and gift.

What I mean to say here is that rationality needs to be complemented and impregnated by contemplation. Max Weber has pointed out how much the modern Western world has become enamoured with rational efficiency.[6] This has been translated into the economics and institutions we have created. And this reflects an understanding of life that has to do with control and productivity, which gives us the idea that we are making it all happen. Our efficiency virtually becomes life's meaning. But there is more to life than this. There is the beauty of art, the mystery of creativity, the profundity of philosophy and the power of religious experience. Life's meaning is not discovered simply by the way we control nature and shape our urbanscape. It is also discovered in contemplation and reflection.

So the meaning of life has to do with living life's giftedness, becoming all that we can be with our capacities, talents and creativities and then bringing that to expression in ways that enrich the wider human community. A lot lies embedded in these few basic statements and these will need further elaboration. One of the critical issues that we will need to look at is what it means to do good in our world and, more basically, what this good looks like. But that is for a later letter.

life's uncertainty

Even though you are young, Naasicaa, you understand that there is nothing smooth about life. Even though life has been good, you have already experienced a fair share of disappointments. There is nothing easy about growing up with parents who are separated, for example. Life is rough, frequently unfair, often difficult, and marked by uncertainty. And while much of life has a sameness about it, there are experiences of pain, sickness and betrayal that rock the foundations of our existence. Victor Hugo is right: 'Hours of ecstasy are never more than a moment'.

I think what we cannot do is hold life's meaning in one hand and life's uncertainty in another, holding all that is secure in the one hand and all that is threatening in the other. It is not quite so neat. Rather, life's meaning includes life's uncertainty. Uncertainty is not an appendix to the main text; it is everywhere throughout the story. Put differently, death is not the footnote to life; death is an integral part of life. Its fine print is already etched onto a baby's fragile hands. The Australian novelist, Morris West, puts it better: 'We are conceived without consent, wrenched whimpering into an alien universe with our death sentence already written on the palms of our helpless hands'.

When I am speaking about uncertainty you must not think that I referring to a pessimistic or negative approach to life. I don't believe that uncertainty needs to lead to cynicism. One can love and embrace life and still recognize and experience its uncertainty. One can commit oneself to friendships and still accept that some relationships will not work out. One can work in the world to bring about change and accept that there may be unintended consequences. Life's uncertainty need not freeze us to inaction, but it can make us less triumphalistic and more careful.

Life is complex and is bigger than each of us. There is much that is out of our hands. And while we act into life seeking to create our structures of security and well-being, life also acts upon us. To put that more clearly, we seek to impact others, but others also impact us. And that is always for both good and ill. While we may seek only to bless others, we will also end up hurting them, and this is also true of the way that others act towards us.

Uncertainty is not only a factor in our interpersonal relationships, but also in the movement of history. Much happens in our world that we do not expect or anticipate. Uncertainty is a key characteristic of much of contemporary life. Economic realities and the job market are as much marked by uncertainty as by predictability. And while some wish to speak about the patterns of history, I think that Jacques Ellul is closer to the mark with his comments about life's arbitrariness.[7]

While we are fed the myth of security and safety by the purveyors of contemporary capitalism, our daily lives are much more fraught by uncertainty. Little wonder that anxiety characterizes the modern psyche and that the therapeutic culture is therefore a hallmark of the West. Without a therapist one almost falls into non-being.

It takes courage to live life. And life's meaning is not found in a single book or a university course. It is found in the living of life in gratitude and hope in the face of the pain and difficulties that come our way. I think the Latin American proverb is appropriate: 'We make our path by walking it'. So much of life is just like that.

the doing of good and the persistence of evil

letter four

It has become more and more difficult in our contemporary world to speak about what's 'good' and the nature of 'evil'. This is due to a whole lot of reasons. But the more obvious ones have to do with the breakdown of traditional communities with their traditions of particular values and the relativism that characterizes our modern mindset.

I am quite sure that it is obvious to you, Naasicaa, that our understanding of and lack of clarity about the one very much affects the other. If we are not sure what the good is, then the nature of evil can also become blurred and vice versa. The other difficulty, particularly now that we are living in a 'global village', is that what one culture or community calls good another regards as wrong. For example, a Palestinian suicide bomber is regarded as a hero in his or her community, while in other parts of the world this is regarded as an act of mindless terrorism. Or a less severe example: in some Asian countries the maintenance of relationship and the 'saving of face' takes priority over truth telling, while in Western culture this would be seen as moral compromise.

In saying this, I am not implying that what is good or evil can always be divided into neat packages. There are gradations of both good and evil. For example, it is good to care for another person, but to give your life in the place of another, as St. Alban the British saint did centuries ago, is a more profound act of goodness. You are also aware that we often speak of the greater good. This usually implies that someone's sacrifice can lead to the benefit of the many. The old analogy here is where some jump or are thrown overboard in a life raft that is grossly over crowded. And regarding evil, things are equally complex. The systems of law in most countries recognize the greater and lesser severity of evil and wrongdoing by the degree of punishment that is meted out to the person found guilty before the court.

We both know that the discussion gets even more complicated. For example, what is good in one setting may be evil in another. For example, violence against another person is wrong. But what of situations of war or self-defense? I have always been fascinated by the shift of Dietrich Bonhoeffer from pacifist to activist leading to his involvement in the conspiracy to kill Adolf Hitler.

So even with these brief introductory comments you can see that there is nothing easy about this discussion. But one simply cannot avoid dealing with it.

why good is necessary

It is very understandable that someone might ask, 'Why think about these issues', or, 'Why can't I just be and live my life'? The response to this is simple enough: we don't 'just live', without also having effects on the lives of others and the world around us. Now it is possible to counter this with the comment that I am just 'small fry' and have little influence in the bigger scheme of things. That may be so. But that really agrees with my point, for the implication is that people with influence do have an impact. And to a lesser degree, so do we all, even if that is only on myself, my immediate family and my friends.

So why should I care that I have an effect? Because at the most fundamental level, *care* is intrinsic to a healthy humanity. Not to care does violence to ourselves. It is the embrace of a 'death' rather than the affirmation of life. No longer to care may lead to anti-social behaviours and criminality, and it will always lead to an internal dying. And to care presupposes the good, because to care is to do good.

In this part of my letter I wish to explore the question of why the good is necessary. The answer, I believe, is that without the good, life is not possible. You and I are the product of the goodness of others towards us. The care, love, concern and interest that parents, family, friends, teachers and others have extended towards us is what makes us human and whole.

I believe this is also what makes community and society possible. While we may sometimes think that it's only the structures, institutions and laws that make society, I do not think this is so. By this I do not mean that these realities are not important; they are. But they are to be the vehicles for good. Laws are there to affirm the good. Political institutions are there to empower a people. Schools exist for intellectual, moral and technical formation. Learning means that we are enriched by traditions so that we can become more fully human.

The good, therefore, is not something that happens only at the interpersonal level, such as being kind to my friend. It also occurs at the institutional level. A company can have good working conditions, a good management structure, produce a good product—one that is useful for humanity—and utilize good sales and distribution practices. It also needs to have a sensitive environmental policy. In this example one can see that the good is to have many dimensions in view and not simply certain outcomes.

It seems to me that the understanding and practice of the good lies at the very heart of the moral universe. And while each of us may not quite script it the same way, there are familiar themes. I don't want to control others, but to empower them. I don't want to destroy, but to build up what is wholesome and good. I don't only want to take, but also to give. I don't want to hate and turn away, but to love and embrace. I don't want to exploit but to care, nurture and steward others, communities and the creation.

Much more could be said, but the basic theme is that I want to resist evil and affirm and nurture the good.

Now, this does not mean that *only* good occurs to us and in our world. Nor does it mean that we only do good no matter how much we may desire that. You have already experienced something of the less than good and even the nasty and hurtful. And I will say more about this in exploring how much good is possible in our world. But I want you to know that I feel that my life has been shaped more by goodness than by anything else. As a result, I live with a deep sense of gratefulness. So much has been given!

The surprise in all of this is that goodness does not always come from the expected places. My experience of my family of origin was not particularly happy. I began my early life with an absent father due to World War II and subsequent migration. This skewed me a bit. But throughout my life older men took an interest in me and in that I found much encouragement. In my own family, in the experience of Christian community, in friendships and in places of education, work and service my overwhelming experience has always been that others have cared for and encouraged me. And for me, the experience of backstabbing and betrayal have only ever been a minor note. Of course, I don't want to deny that others may have had quite different experiences to mine.

The many years of working in urban mission with homeless youth, drug addicts, prostitutes and people with serious life-controlling problems never dinted my sense of the goodness of people. While in no way wanting to condone these sorts of behaviours, I again and again found that most of these people were more 'wounded' than bad. And when some of this woundedness was healed, these new companions on the journey enriched our lives and the lives of others. You know that I am not talking theory here, because some of these young people lived in our home when your mother was a child.[1]

the nature of good

While I believe that definitions can be helpful in certain areas of discourse, in others they are most unhelpful. For example, how does one define beautiful, or more specifically a beautiful painting? If I define the good as that which contributes to the sustenance, nurture and development of life, this is a good start, but I don't think it gets us very far. So let me attempt a thicker description.

The old idea that the good is what my conscience dictates is not tenable. The logic that operates in this notion is that somewhere at the core of my being, usually regarded as the soul or the human spirit, there is a perfect set of values. It is something like a divine barometer or alarm clock. In ancient Greek thought this was thought to be the divine spark within humanity. Through the burdens and complexities of life this pure spark gets buried or muddied and so we have to find ways to scrape off 'the gunk' in order to hear this innate goodness and then act on it.

This idea is not credible for many reasons. The first is that it posits an immortal or pure soul which does violence to the reality of our vulnerable humanity. Secondly, it commits us to a subjective internal archaeological expedition. And who is to say that we will ever find this core and not our own delusions? Thirdly, this view means that our experience of life and of the human community can add nothing to our understanding of the good, since the good is innate. There are also serious theological problems with this view, but I won't go into them now except to say that the Reformational view questions the whole notion of an innate goodness in humanity. The main problem with this perspective is that it overlooks the whole process of socialization and moral formation.

Others suggest that the good is what our society believes and teaches its members through family, schooling, media and society's other institutions. That this process takes place is of little doubt. We are shaped by our society and culture. But that the current values of a society should be the measure of the good is also open to serious question. One concern is that societies promote or condone things that are obviously wrong. In the past some societies condoned slavery, and this is still practiced in our modern world.[2] Our present Western societies condone work practices that take little account of impact on families or health, and until recently, showed little concern for the environment. Another concern is that societies tend to be blind to their own psycho-pathologies. Hitler's Germany is a case in point. But so is America's preoccupation with the individualism and violence that fissures its way throughout the culture.[3] A further matter is that modern societies are no longer homogeneous, but ethnically, and therefore often ethically, diverse.

If you are following me in this discussion, then I am saying that one's understanding of the good cannot simply lie innately with the individual, nor can it be solely determined by the dominant values of our society. Our understanding of the good has to transcend both. This means that the good has to be shaped by transcendental values. And we come to those through reflective processes by listening to the voices of historians, philosophers, artists and the religious.

The nature of good, which sustains and nurtures life and well-being, is bigger than each one of us. And to some extent it is a good that is beyond us. In other words, the good is like the winsome voice of a lover, the voice that surprises us and calls us forward and beyond ourselves. The good that brings blessing rather than harm, peace rather than violence, and wholeness rather than fragmentation and dissolution is a good that beckons us. And in its embrace and praxis we ourselves are made more whole.

What all of this means is that the good, the being and the doing of good, cannot be separated from the movement to love and to hope. In fact, to do the good can only spring from the desire and capacity to love. And the continuation of the good has to be borne on the wings of hope.

I think that the greatest good comes to expression not in heroic individualism but in the context of community.[4] That is the place where we learn to do good to each other and seek to extend that good to the wider community.

good for whom?

One of the things that we need to think about, Naasicaa, is that so often in our contemporary culture, when we think of the good we think only of what is good *for me.* Or to put that on a much grander scale, what is good for America is assumed to be good for the rest of the world. Hence we need to ask this question: good for whom?

It is very apparent when one lives in Asia that the Asian mindset is very different to that of the West. The general orientation is not what is best *for me,* but what is best *for us.* And this usually means the family and extended family and sometimes also the wider community. This way of thinking and living is largely lost in Western societies. And we see this particularly in the loss of commitment to the common social good. We want social systems and institutions to work for us. We are prepared to give little back.

A member of a Western family does not make life and vocational choices with the benefit of the family in view. In fact, it is the other way round. The family is expected to be a resource to help me in becoming and doing what I want to be.

Similarly, employees think about their career path in a company and give little thought to how they may benefit the company. Or again, a student attends a particular graduate school to enhance his or her career or ministry with little thought of contributing to the school. Hence student associations cannot fill the various positions to serve the wider student body.

What I am referring to is the self-interest that characterizes people in our contemporary Western societies. This is individualism elevated to the status of a right and a demand. The sad implication of all of this is that others are there only for me. I have no responsibility for them. This is fundamentally abusive and tears apart the fabric of a civil society.

I believe that for something to be good, it can't be good *only* for me. It must also be good for others. One of the things I have really appreciated about the thinking and strategy of Martin Luther King, Jr. was his emphasis that not only did the African-American need liberation, but so did the white oppressor. Both victim and perpetrator needed to be set free.[5] Thus true freedom is not for the one at the cost of the other, but freedom for all. And to the extent that others are not free, I am not free. Or to put that differently, if I am blessed but others are not, then I am not truly blessed.

One implication of this is that when others suffer, I also suffer. We see this particularly in close relationships. A parent may grieve deeply over the waywardness of one's child. A lover hurts deeply when the loved one is hurt or taken away in death. But we need to see this more broadly as well. I can't be happy as a politician when my people suffer. And I can't be satisfied as a business person when some of my employees are exploited. Thus profit-making cannot be the only criteria for a good business. Goodness is always a wider configuration.

And yet the notion seems to persist that what is good is what is good *for me.* So we see party politics which have little to do with the national good. We have business practices that favour the profitability of the corporation but misuse people. And we experience relationships that are exploitative and sometimes abusive. So what does it mean when someone says 'I love you' but is emotionally or sexually exploitative? What does it mean when parents say they love and care for their children, but are emotionally absent or are manipulative and controlling? Well, it doesn't mean much. The good is absent. We do a 'snow job' on the good despite the abundance of our stated intentions and many words. Good, therefore, cannot be merely at the level of intentionality. Good is a form of praxis.

What I am saying is that the good is not my personal property and privilege. It is something that we have together, if we have it at all. In Western culture, we no longer understand this very well; we think that we need to carve out the good for ourselves. So some live the 'good life' by living in exclusive condos with electric gates and antiseptic streets. But this is not the good life. It is a diminished life. It is sterile in its very opulence. Exclusivity is the self-interested protection of the good from its real humanity and, therefore, from its authenticity.

After working for many years with troubled young people from 'the wrong side of the tracks', as the Americans would say, I needed a break. So for six months I worked for my father-in-law to clean the houses of the rich. And not to my surprise I discovered many unhappy, isolated and drug-addicted wealthy people—so lonely, in fact, that some paid me to drink coffee and talk with them rather than do their house cleaning.

Having lived in a Third World country, the Philippines, it is obvious that the good in our global world is still seen as what is good for the West. So while the old exploitative colonialism is dead, First World exploitation of the Third World is alive and well in spite of all the rhetoric about rich countries helping the poorer ones.

There is much more to say about all of this, but letters have their limits and so has your reading concentration. The good is what blesses *all* of us, not simply the well off. In fact, I will later develop the idea that the good blesses the poor and weak. What all of this means is that doing good brings with it a cost. Good is not cheap and to do good may well cost us much. It is usually a call to downward mobility.[6]

how much good is possible?

In one way or another, I have thought about this issue most of my life. There are two factors at play here. The one is that as an activist, I have worked, together with others, hard and long to bring about certain social changes, particularly in the field of drug abuse. While we may have done some good, the basic reality was that things simply got worse, not better. In mid-flight of all that activity, I sometimes became deeply discouraged, wondering what was the point of going on. I want you to know this, Naasicaa, so you will realize that I don't have nice and neat answers. The other factor is that I teach a graduate course that deals with theories and strategies for social transformation. Here I am supposed to have answers, but I have grave doubts about much of the thinking in this area.

I do wonder whether I think about these issues differently depending on where I am. In the slums of Manila, despite the persistence of poverty, people inspired me with hope. Not only did much good take place in the most difficult of life's circumstances, but people continued to live, believe and act in hope that the greater good is possible. I don't experience that same sense of hope amongst the street people of East Vancouver. Instead, I sense resignation and bitterness. People simply feel abandoned by the system. Good will never come to them, it seems.

Last year while in Yangon, Myanmar, I was also wrestling with this question of how much good is possible in a country that is suffering under an oppressive military dictatorship and in dire poverty. In connecting up with some of my former Burmese students and seeing their work for transformation on the outskirts of Yangon, I both rejoiced and wept. I rejoiced at their courage to improve the lot of others, but almost despaired regarding the insurmountable odds and the relentless poverty I saw.

So I really don't know how much good is possible in our world. Sometimes I feel like saying 'not much'. At other times, I am more hopeful.

I think we have to acknowledge that while there is much good in our world, there is also much that is evil and unjust. And the latter just does not go away, hence my reference to the persistence of evil. The problem is that evil does not only lie out there with the 'baddies', it also lies close at hand for all of us. In fact, it lies within. I believe that we were made to be and do good, but we are very capable of wrongdoing.

Evil can be described as the absence of the good. What this means is that I not only do wrong when I harm someone, but also when I neglect someone. It is evil to oppress a people. It is equally evil to neglect people.

As far as I have been able to understand these difficult matters, I think that much evil and wrongdoing comes from those who have first been wronged, harmed and abused. Thus we talk of the cycle of abuse. The abused become the abusers. I also think that evil comes from the misuse of power. The greater one's power, the greater the responsibility and the greater the opportunity to do good. But power does corrupt and often instead of using this power *for* and *on behalf* of others, this power is used for *oneself* and *against* others.[7]

Furthermore, while wrongdoing occurs at the personal level, it also occurs at the structural level. Here we speak about structural evil. What we mean by this is that evil can become embodied and embedded in social and cultural values and society's institutions.[8] Slavery was a form of structural evil yet was regarded as a normal part of the society of that time. And the present day persistence of a patriarchy that oppresses and marginalizes women is similarly a form of structural evil.

I do not believe, Naasicaa, that good will fully triumph in our present world. Nor do I believe that evil will triumph. The lesson of history is that while evil may reign long, the seeds of decay are within it, and it eventually comes undone. At the same time, the movements of good also carry the seeds of death and will deteriorate. The good must therefore be won again and again in the face of evil.

I see a lot of good in you, Naasicaa. I believe that you will want to do good in our world and not do harm. To live like this will require a lot of courage and deep inner strength and resources. You will need to understand and tap those resources. And about that we will need to talk some more later.

the story of god and the human predicament

letter five

It's five a.m. The Manila sun is already making its way through the polluted heavens, giving it a more subdued colour. It's as if a fine see-through shroud has enveloped the world. Along with many others, I am in the Roman Catholic Church of the Sacred Heart, joining the faithful in worship, adoration and the eucharist. There is nothing outstanding about the liturgy, but I always sense a presence in this old building with its cool stone floors, its porticoes open to the street already bursting with jeepneys, tricycles, hundreds of people and the vendors making an early beginning to a long day of probably small pickings. Birds irreverently flutter in and out, while beggar children reverently wait for the service to end to accost the faithful to share the fruits of their spirituality through the practice of charity.

Later, after having had breakfast, I walk to the Protestant seminary where I teach. I am not at all sure what

my colleagues think about my early morning escapades
to the Roman Catholic Church. But to be honest, I don't
care too much. I always come away feeling blessed through
having been in God's presence. And I am quite sure that God
is not too impressed with all of our 'man'-made divisions
and distinctions within the church.

But it is not my intention to talk about the church.
I will do that later. I do want to talk about God and 'his'
presence in the world. And even though I began this letter
by speaking about experiencing God in church, I in no way
want to suggest that God can only be experienced there.
God is not limited in that way. Nor should we think that the
experience of God is only a churchly activity. This kind of
thinking has led to a huge divide in Western thinking, where
we separate the sacred and the secular. God is thought to be
there for the Sunday experience, but is somehow irrelevant
from Monday to Saturday.[1] This has made the church a
religious ghetto and has left the life of work and play without
any sacred dimensions.

I believe that God can be present to us in all the
dimensions of life: in our praying and playing; in work and
in contemplation; in liturgy and nature; in mission and
politics; in preaching and art. God's presence is relevant to
the *whole* of life and not simply to some narrow religious
segment.

god as problematic

But I can already see you shaking your head, Naasicaa.
And I can hear you saying, 'But wait a minute, how can
you speak so confidently about God when God is such a
problematic idea in our world?' You are right, of course.
God is a difficult 'idea' in contemporary Western culture.

This is so for several reasons. One is the long
Enlightenment project, where Western thinkers began

to question the authority and tradition of the church and ended up replacing the church's claim to knowledge based on revelation with the counter claim of knowledge based on human reason. The outworking of this, even up to the present day, is the idea that 'real' facts are the product of science and that 'soft' facts, including matters of faith and spirituality, belong to the sphere of personal opinion.[2] This of course means that while matters of science are certain, matters of religious faith are not. They are simply personal values that some people hold. As a result, we don't really mind if someone deeply believes in God. That is his or her personal business. It has nothing to do with me if I happen to believe that God is simply a fanciful idea.

There are several problems with this confident Enlightenment idea. The first is that we are no longer so sure, following the work of Thomas Kuhn amongst others, that science simply gives us facts. Science also gives us traditions of interpretation just as philosophy, history and religion.[3] And secondly, the story of God is not my personal idea. Someone can't say, 'Oh, you just sucked that idea out of your thumb!' The story of God is a public story. It is a long story. And it is a story addressed to all of humanity. So the story cannot be reduced to one's subjective values. It belongs to the realm of general discourse.

Another factor that has made the idea of God problematical is the thesis expressed by Feuerbach, amongst others, that 'God' is simply a projection of our own needs and insecurities. This means that God is not really there. God is mere wish-fulfillment.[4] Given my smallness and vulnerability in a big and complex world and given the inevitability of death, it is not surprising that I want to resist and transcend these realities. As a result, human beings have 'invented' God. God is everything that we are not. We are finite; God is infinite. We are often powerless; God is all powerful. We fail and mess things up; God forgives, heals and makes all things new.

I think that Feuerbach is right in identifying that we 'need' God. But it does not follow that we therefore 'invent' God. I need love, but this does not necessarily mean I therefore live in love's make-believe world. I believe that we should turn Feuerbach upside down. Our need for God is because we have been made in God's image and made for relationship with God, just as we have been created to love and be loved. The book of Ecclesiastes puts it rather nicely: God has set eternity in the hearts of humanity.

There is another factor as well. In our world as 'global village' and in a climate of pluralism, it is little wonder that we ask the question, 'Which God are we talking about?' Is it the 'god' of Islam, the Jewish faith, Hinduism, Christianity, or that of the primal religions of First Nations peoples? Are there, then, many 'gods'? Or is there the one God who manifests 'himself' in various ways in the differing religious traditions?[5]

It is obvious that there are many gods, including the contemporary gods of our own making. Here we may define god as something to which we give our ultimate allegiance. It is interesting how we now speak of the gods of sport, referring to our sporting heroes. And since greed has been proclaimed as good in Western culture, material acquisition is another contemporary god.[6] So whether ancient or modern, there have always been many gods. But are they all differing manifestations of the One God? I think not. If that were the case, this god would be scary and I would certainly never give my allegiance to such a god. The reason I say this is because the gods are contradictory. So how can we be confident about a god who gives us conflicting messages about who 'he' is? The gods of primal religions, of Hinduism and of our contemporary culture are very different to the God of the biblical story. So somewhere along the line we have to choose whom we will love, worship and serve. There is nothing flippant about this choice. It is a painful one, particularly because our culture tells us that we are intolerant if we make such a choice.

Taken together, all of these issues make the notion of God very difficult. I believe the church itself has not helped either. It has become a defensive institution. It has fostered a dualism that makes God irrelevant to much of life and has often failed to live up to its own message. But I will come back to this when I write to you about the church.

god as actor in history

I won't try to deal any further with all of these difficulties, but will come back to them in later letters. Nor do I wish to talk speculatively about God. I am not all that sure that expressions such as 'God as Ultimate Other' or 'God as ground of our Being' get us very far. Instead, I wish to talk about the story of God as told in Judeo-Christian tradition. It is the story of a God who joins us in the human fray. It is this God who has captured my heart and imagination.

The story of God is a long story. The story of Abraham may go back to nearly two thousand years BC and what led up to that story goes back into the hoary mists of time. This long story has been believed and lived over the many centuries of Israel's history in both good and bad times. Therefore, there is nothing trite or simplistic about this story. It is not a one-day wonder. If you like, it has withstood the painful rigours of time.

It is also a colourful story. The story like that of the Exodus is told in dramatic prose. That of the book of Isaiah is told with visionary prophecy. The Psalms are the heart and prayer language of the Old Testament, and Proverbs, as wisdom literature, provides us with a picture of what it means to live a life that pleases God and blesses the

neighbour. There is, therefore, nothing monochrome about
the Bible. And its literary power makes it one of the great
books of all time.[7] If truth be known, it should be on the
New York Times best seller list each week, for it far outsells
any other book each year.

But the heart of the matter does not simply lie in its
literary power. Rather, it lies in the fact that the God of
the Bible has come amongst us. This is not the God of
philosophical speculation. Nor the God of the sole mystic
who has some visionary experience unattainable to other
mere mortals. Nor is it the God of holy remoteness: a
deistic God moving the wheels of destiny, but far removed
from the beauty and pain of the human condition and the
paradoxical movement of history.

The story of God is the story of the Exodus. It is a story of
liberation.[8] It tells of a God who hears the cry of 'his' people's
suffering and who comes to their aid against the Pharaohs
of this world. It's the story of movement from ignomy and
marginalization to promise and rescue. At heart, it is the
story of freedom. Little wonder that theologians have seen
redemption and freedom as central to the whole biblical
message.

But this story of God's care for Israel is embedded in
a much larger story. For the God of Israel is no parochial
tribal deity, but the God who made the heavens and earth.
This God is not only the God of a particular history and of a
particular people, but of the whole earth and of all humanity.
And Israel's blessing in knowing this God was not simply
for itself. They were to be a light to all the nations. God does
not have the few in view, but all. God is not the God of a
particular time, but of all history and into the eschaton.

This larger story encapsulates the themes of creation,
the fall into chaos and the surprise of recreation. God's
world is 'his' artwork. God the great designer calls into
being a world of astounding beauty. And into this world,

with all its residual potentiality and resources, 'he' places the creatures most like 'himself'—woman and man. Made in God's image, humans are made for God, for each other and for participation in the world. What this means is that we are fundamentally relational beings and we have a calling to shape the world. That this grand story got 'messed up' is the sad fact of the human endeavour. Our foolish pride led to rebellion and alienation. The result was every form of distortion. Our relationship with God, each other and with the created order suffered. The first good news is that God made all things good. The second good news is that our messing things up is *not* the final word. God comes to help us, to make us 'new'. God desires to restore all things.

Every story has its implications. So has this story. One important matter is that God and the world cannot be totally opposed to each other. It is not true that God is only good while the world is wholly bad. This is an unacceptable dualism. What is true is that God is eternal and the world is a creation. Therefore the world and what is in it cannot be God. As a result, things and people should not be worshipped. Only God is worthy of our worship and obedience. But this does mean that the world is wholly good. Human folly and disobedience have brought about a distortion in the order of things and even nature itself has become affected. But God is *for* the world. God made it, sustains it and is recreating all things. And God invites us to join 'him' in caring for all of creation. Thus to do good in our world is to join with God in 'his' love for the world.

Another important element in the story is the rescue that God seeks to achieve. We find this idea difficult because we don't like the fact that we need others to help us. This is an affront to our ability and independence. But it is obvious that we are interdependent creatures. The very fabric of society reflects this. We need parents, teachers, friends, farmers, manufacturers, systems experts, medical personel. The list is endless. So what is so difficult then about our needing God? What is so difficult about living in the presence of a God who made us, joins us in the journey of life, forgives our sins and stupidities, heals our woundedness and empowers us to live life in full stride?[9] God does not seek to diminish us, but to lead us to wholeness and purpose. To live *with* God deepens our humanity. And to live *for* God is to do God's recreative good in our world. And that involves our engagement in all of life and not simply participation in religious activity.

I have often wondered what vocation you will choose, Naasicaa. Both your mother and your maternal grandmother have a strong artistic bent. Maybe you will follow in their footsteps? So your vocation may choose you, rather than the other way round? I believe that God is the consummate artist and your possible move in that vocational direction may be a small reflection of the passion of God. This is not to say that God is only spoken of as artist, but also as vine dresser, architect, healer, shepherd.[10] The descriptive metaphors[11] about God are numerous and so is the scope of human activity, all of which can be done by cooperating with God to bless our world.

god as trinity

When we think about God we often think about a God or the God. We don't think too much about God as Trinity. Yet throughout the biblical story we hear of God as Father, Son and Holy Spirit. This may not seem all that important to you, but I think it is.

Your aunty, Marina, when she was a young girl, was quite convinced that the Bible didn't get that quite right. She always spoke of God as Father, Mother and Son. She thought that was a much more logical order. But maybe she was also questing for the feminine in God? That, however, is a whole other story, and we will come back to that at another time.

God as Trinity does not mean that there are three Gods. There is the one God, but this God has three modes of existence or God expresses 'himself' in three ways. In God there is unity in diversity. Or to put that differently, God is a community of 'persons'. Augustine sought to express this mystery as God as Lover, Beloved and Love itself. In more recent theological thinking we speak of God the Father as the architect, creator, builder and sustainer of all things; God the Son as the redeemer, reconciler, healer and restorer of humanity and of all things fractured in our world; and God the Holy Spirit as the beautifier, empowerer, inspirer and revealer to all of humanity in its quest for love and renewal.[12]

The reason why it is so important to think about the Trinity is that so often we become one-sided and reductionistic in our understanding of God. Some only want to think about God as Creator. This, however, leaves God as powerful, but remote. Others only want to emphasize God as Redeemer in Christ and so speak of God's salvation, healing and forgiveness. While this rightly emphasizes personal transformation we must not lose the larger picture from view. God wishes to bless not only individuals, but also families, communities, neighbourhoods and the world as a whole. Others again wish to focus on the mysterious work of the Holy Spirit in bringing gifts and graces into our lives and bringing inspiration and revelation. But this if stressed one-sidedly can lead us into other-worldly mysticism.

God as Trinity reminds us that creation, redemption and renewal belong together. This affirms the world, calls for the transformation of all that is evil and reminds us that God empowers and graces us to live in this world. God as Trinity reminds us that building the wider community, building the community of faith and having sources of inspiration all belong together. It reminds us that the world of politics and work, the world of evangelization and mission, and the world of prayer and contemplation belong to each other.

It is very sad that some churches have inadvertently dismembered the Trinity. Some mainly speak about God's concern for the created world and as a result focus only on environmental theology. Others mainly emphasize God's redemptive activity and focus only on Christology. Others still emphasize spiritual renewal, but have little concern for the wider social issues and the work of justice and social transformation.

I would like to draw some implications from this important part of the story of God. The first, in the words of the Cappadocian Fathers, is that the 'members' of the Trinity are committed to mutual care and self-giving in a communion of love and this is of significance for us. For if God participates in this movement of self-giving, or to put it differently, in the rhythm of reciprocity, then this calls us, who are made in God's image, to do likewise. The contemporary values of self-fulfilment and independence are therefore very far off the mark. The very nature of God calls us to live a very different rhythm of life—one of mutual care, giving and receiving.

The other implication, embedded in the first, is that if God is a community of 'persons', then we too are called to the community-building task. The nuture of family, friendships, communities of faith, partnerships in the workplace and hospitality in our neighbourhoods is the creative and demanding task to which we are all invited. And in attempting to fulfil this task, we reflect something of the being of God.

I think you can see in this discussion that God as Trinity is not abstract theological thinking, but has ramifications for the way we live now.

the long march of god

I hope, Naasicaa, that you will read the story of God for yourself. It's an amazing story. It begins in the faded mists of time with the beginnings of our world. It then moves from the general story of earth's primal history to the personal story of Abraham, to the story of the Exodus and conquest, to the emergence of the nation of Israel called to live in covenant with the God who had redeemed them.

The story traces the move from Israel's tribal confederacy to the rule of kings and the growing power and wealth of this small nation jammed in between the superpowers of that time. And in this development we see played out most of the issues that still plague us today. We see those in power, called to serve and bless the people, misuse their power for personal ends. We see the growing gap between rich and poor. And we see people initially awestruck by the presence of God in their midst become tired of the long road of obedience. This results in the hunger for other gods, the gods of their own making, and the resulting social consequence of covenant-breaking, which in turn leads to lack of care for the neighbour.

This basic story has repeated itself in the course of history. Peoples blessed by God have taken things for granted; faith has waned and deterioration has set in. This is true today in the deterioration of the Christian faith in the Western world. In the 1800s more than eighty percent of Christians in the world were from Western nations. Today in many European countries, Christians are a tiny minority, while more than sixty percent of Christians in the world today come from the Third World.

But this basic story is often also our own personal story. We begin the journey of faith in love and hope and with great enthusiasm. But we become discouraged, get side-tracked and lose our way. Faith gives way to doubt and faithfulness succumbs to disobedience.

What's remarkable in this story is the persistent action of God. God neither washes 'his' hands to withdraw from our mess nor ever gives up. God sends prophets to call us to faithfulness and to a new vision of the reign of God and provides priests to bring healing to our lives. And God calls 'his' people back to covenant faithfulness and to the kingly role of reflecting God's lordship in the world.

This pattern of the movement from enthusiasm to faithlessness and from judgment to renewal brings us to the story of Jesus. Jesus came to bring renewal to a tired Judaism, to proclaim a fuller vision of the kingdom of God and to call the social outcasts to God's banqueting table.[13]

In the story of Jesus we see the long march of God to bring hope and healing to his people and to the whole world. In this story of the carpenter's 'son' we see the amazing movement of God to visibility and vulnerability. God as infinite and eternal being comes amongst us in Jesus Christ. This is the miracle of incarnation. It is not humans climbing the mystical ladder to find God, nor humans probing inward to discover an unsullied immortality, but it is God bending down towards us in tears of compassion and the pain of identification. Mother Teresa speaks about being kissed by God.[14]

Jesus comes as the messenger of God, calling people to repentance and renewal. He heals the sick and performs exorcisms. He builds a community of disciples of women and men and empowers them to become part of his mission. The heart of that mission is sharing the love, forgiveness and generosity of God to all, including the poor. Jesus seeks to bring about a revolution of the heart, which brings love, peace and justice into a world marked by suspicion and inequality.

The continuing story-line is a familiar one. People are enthusiastic about the good news that Jesus brings, but there is opposition by religious leaders who are threatened and offended by the message of Jesus. And at the end of the day enthusiasm wanes and is replaced by abandonment and betrayal. Jesus, Son of Man and Son of God, shares the fate of criminals and is crucified. The one who came to serve had to give his very life.

But the story of God is never a story where evil triumphs and where we have the last word. Remember, Naasicaa, how I pointed out earlier that God does not give up? And in the places of deepest darkness, 'his' light shines. The story of the cross becomes the story of the resurrection, where the bands of death are broken and Jesus appears to the shattered community of his followers to inspire them with the victory of God, the renewal of hope and the empowerment of the Spirit.

The story of Jesus becomes the story of the early church. Inspired by the One who loved unto death and who in his death carries our folly, sin and shame and bequeaths forgiveness and healing, the early Christians followed in the footsteps of their Lord. They formed communities to worship God and celebrate the eucharist, and they sought to live contrary to the pervasive values of the then-known world.[15]

It is at this point that the story of God partly becomes the story of the church: with its long decades of persecution, the eventual Christianization of the Roman world, the later evangelization of barbaric 'Europe' from the sixth to the eleventh centuries, the fascinating development of monasticism from the fourth century onwards, the growing power of the popes and the collusion of church and state, the Reformation, the evangelization of newfound peoples in other parts of the globe, and the colonization project leading to the church in the modern world under attack from rationalism and science.[16] This story I will have to tell in some more detail later. But it is important to note that even though the story of God becomes the story of the church, the story of God continues. God is not limited to the church. God continues to work in our world and challenges 'his' people to renewal by the Spirit.

the human predicament

The story of God is not simply about God. It is also the story of the world, humanity, and the world to come. It is therefore a big story. At the heart of the story is God's good purposes for our world and for us as human beings. What gives the story such poignancy is that while God seeks to grace us with good gifts so that we can live wholesome and blessed lives, we seldom like God's way with us. Basically, we want to live life our own way. So the God who could force, but has chosen the way of gentle nudging, ever seeks to draw us into 'his' will and purpose for our lives.

The great human predicament is that we were made for relationship with God, but God is frequently neglected or relegated to the sidelines of our lives and our world. Furthermore, if we don't want to live lives centred in God, then we soon create our own centre-points. Or to put that differently, we create our own idols. The irony of all of this is that we therefore don't ever get away from being creatures who worship something and someone. But why worship what we have made when we may worship the God who has given us life and gifts and makes all things possible?

I wonder, Naasicaa, how you are approaching life? You are probably looking to the future with a great deal of hope and enthusiasm. You have plans regarding what you hope to be and what you will do. In many ways you are facing an open future. So much is possible and achievable in our kind of world. And you are empowered in that you have many options and opportunities. So you are blessed. You know that this is not true of many others in our world, where poverty and oppression have closed the door to a more open future.

So in all of this, what and who will be the source of your life's inspiration? This is an important question. For we are not only outwardly constrained in the ways that life places all sorts of limits on us, but we are also inwardly motivated. So the question is, what moves, motivates and inspires you? Exploring this question brings us again to the human predicament. For we are often mixed up in what we do. We do things because they are right and good, but we also try to please others and we want things for ourselves and we may need to be needed.

Knowing our more central inspiration is one thing, but this is so often overlaid with fears, self-doubt and insecurities. We are far more fragile and vulnerable than we make out.[17] And there is the added problem that others don't believe in us or encourage us, so we are pushed down rather than built up. Not everyone around us is committed to our well-being, so we need to be discerning about who we will listen to, who will inspire us and who will mentor us.

To conclude this letter, I think the human predicament is that often we don't know what we should live for, to whom we can entrust ourselves or how we can do good in our world. I think that this can bring us back to the story of God. To entrust ourselves to the wisdom and grace of God and to do God's good in our world, can be the central inspiration to the whole of our lives.

faith and doubt in a perilous world

letter six

I still remember with great clarity our months on Mt. Tamborine inland from Queensland's Gold Coast. A good friend of ours had made available a pine cottage for a time of recuperation when we returned to Australia from years of service in the Philippines. Cold nights were spent in front of an open fire place. Days were spent wandering in the subtropical rainforests that had survived the push of development. But the idyllic setting was not the state of our hearts. We were in the midst of uncertainty. And once again, we were at a major transition point in our lives.

How different our lives have been to that of my parents after they migrated to Australia. My father lived in the same house, attended the same church and pursued one area of work. He did business with the same bank, petrol station and garage. His has been a life of regularity and continuity.

We had returned from the Philippines without any clarity as to what we would do once we were back in Australia. One chapter of our lives had closed. The other was still to be written. And the page was blank. In these kinds of transition points, faith and doubt co-mingle and run the risk of coagulation. Faith speaks of the hope that something will open up and work out. Doubt speaks the language of uncertainty and fear: there may be no future for us; this may be the end of employment and service. I don't know about you, but I think this movement of faith and doubt is very much a part of the human condition.

life's dialectic

You will have noticed, Naasicaa, that in my letters so far I never mention one theme without also referring to another that seems to be the opposite. So here I speak about faith and doubt. In the previous letter I spoke about the story of God and the human predicament. In a future letter I plan to speak about the sign and contradiction of the community of faith.

The reason I do this is because I believe that we cannot think about life in other terms. We cannot really talk about love without talking about indifference, or equally bad, about the power of hate. And faith cannot be reasonably discussed without probing the realities of doubt. Moreover, the two conditions cannot be wholly separated, for one cannot have faith without having doubted.

What I am talking about here is life's strange dialectic. I am not particularly referring to Hegel's paradigm of thesis, antithesis and synthesis nor agreeing with his notion of the movement of history to Absolute Spirit.[1] I think that is both a too-neat categorization and a too-neat idealization of the complexity of history. I am referring to the paradoxical nature of life and how polarities occur, leading to new forms of understanding and integration. For example, when a major paradigm shift occurs in science or philosophy it is never wholly new, never an obvious extension of the old, but frequently an incorporation of elements of the old with the new.

At the same time, I am referring to the fact that life cannot be reduced to singularities and neat categorizations. Max Weber has rightly noted how Western thinking always moves to rationalization and systems.[2] And Kierkegaard has signalled the either/or orientation of our philosophical mindset.[3] But we both know that systems have inner systems and create counter-systems and that often the question is not either/or but both/and.

I am also referring to the fact that so much of what we do in society has different and unintended consequences. By engaging in certain strategies we hope to achieve certain outcomes. But things don't always work the way we had hoped. In fact, sometimes we achieve the opposite of what we intended. Jacques Ellul is right in noting that many liberation movements in the modern world have only brought about greater oppression. He is also critical of the way in which we have attempted to manipulate our world while failing to realize that we were at the same time reshaping our own inner consciousness.[4] I think we see these difficulties at the interpersonal level as well. We seek to be kind, but often end up spoiling the other person. We seek to help certain communities and groups of people and end up making them more dependent rather than empowering them. It seems that our attempts to do good don't always have good outcomes.

In Christian thought we also find a dialectic and the movement of reversal. The prosperity of Israel leads to decay, and the severe mercy displayed to Job leads to deeper faith. The experience of Israel in the desert is the place of purgation. The death of Christ issues in the resurrection.

The social power of the church leads to the loss of dynamic faith and the church in times of persecution spawns martyrs and renews its life and faith. In places of academic sophistication, theology has become sterile while in the slums of the Third World, new liberation theologies are born.[5] I remember in the 1960s, while the theologians were pronouncing the God-is-dead theology, thousands of young people were caught up in the Jesus Movement and came to a living faith.[6]

In the experience of spirituality we find a similar set of paradoxes. In our certainties we can become rigid; in our doubts we can find renewed hope; and in our emptiness we may discover the very blessings of God. In the practice of asceticism, while living with less, we somehow gain more.[7] And in grief and suffering we find not only comfort, but sometimes a whole new vision for the future.

All of this sounds somewhat strange. It is as if we cannot draw a straight line from point A to point B. Our culture, however, tells us something quite different. It constantly reminds us that we can get what we want. If we do this type of university course we will get a good job. If we use these kinds of products we will be well and happy. If we achieve these outcomes we will be successful. Our society tells us that we can be in control and that we can draw straight lines.

But I think that life is much more happenstance. I am not suggesting that we live passively awaiting our fate. It is important to plan. It is also important to pray. But there is a mysterious quality to life and we need to be open to the God of surprises.

general faith and doubt

Faith means to have trust and confidence in someone or something. I trust that the university lecturer will mark my paper fairly. And I have confidence that the train, as indicated in the timetable, will stop at all stations.

Faith is not a strange dimension in our lives. It is the bread and butter, or in the language of other cultures, the rice and fish, of life. I, therefore, always find it very strange that people want to scoff at the idea of faith. They give the impression that faith somehow means that one has lost the ability to think clearly or one is some religious fanatic. But life is not sustainable if faith and trust are absent.

As you well know, Naasicaa, we all begin the journey of life trusting others, particularly the significant others in our lives—parents, siblings, extended family members and friends. We also trust the institutions and services in the wider community. And if we have doubts in our earlier years it usually has to do with self-doubt. We wonder whether we are good enough, smart enough and beautiful or handsome enough. And the answer that we usually give ourselves is 'no', we are not. This is a problem that we will need to discuss at another time.

As we grow into our teenage years we begin to question things. Our naive trust will have been wounded. And hopefully we will begin to grow towards a more mature trust. We no longer so readily take things at face value. We are more careful and more critical. So there is not only faith but also doubt. Mature trust is one that has stopped to listen carefully to doubt's call, has processed that call and has moved forward. Faith and doubt are both necessary. The idea that faith is good and doubt is bad is clearly nonsense. One might as well say that daylight is good and darkness is bad. The only thing that is bad, as far as I can see, is that we have a naïve faith and spawn a cynical doubt. The one makes us blind to real evil. The other makes us deaf to genuine good.

So what I am pointing out is that faith and doubt are part of the normal rhythm of life. Faith makes us open to others and to opportunities. Doubt makes us halt long enough to question and possibly reconsider. Faith helps us to participate and join. Doubt helps us to disconnect. Both movements are important. And surprisingly, doubt actually serves faith. If I want to move ahead but I have stopped long enough to question and explore my doubts and concerns and I decide to proceed, faith will be stronger for having doubted.

I think we do need to talk about the sources of faith and doubt. Here we enter the whole complex discussion of how we know something. Do I trust someone or something because I have facts or experience or intuition? Or is it a combination of all three? This is difficult to answer. The 'facts' of the case may have put a person on death row but each year some cases are overturned and people are found to be innocent. I may have seriously doubted whether a particular person was right for the job. But it turns out that he or she is an excellent employee. Or conversely, I may have had a hunch that something would work out, but in fact it didn't. I was mistaken.

All of this invites us into the complexity and mystery of life. Things are often less than sure. And things are not always as they seem. We know less than what we think. And we can make mistakes as much as we may get things right.

Naasicaa, if there is anything that I wish to say directly to you at this point, it is simply that you take time with the issues and decisions of your life. Don't jump into major decisions through external constraints or inner compulsions. Take time to wait, time to weigh things up. In other words, become a contemplative.[8] What I mean by that is not that you become a monk, but that you take time to be still, to pray and hear what you should do. I am not talking about receiving handwriting on the wall, but

hearing the handwriting on the fragile texture of your soul
and carefully evaluating the circumstances of your life.

religious faith and doubt

There are people who believe that these two words—
faith and doubt—do not belong together in religious
language. Only faith does. They regard doubt as something
negative, maybe even evil. I don't agree with this viewpoint,
and hopefully it will become clear when I attempt to
explain why I think this way.

In the language of Christianity, when we speak about
faith we usually mean two things. We speak of *the* faith,
and by this we mean the *content* of faith, and we speak
of *having* faith or trust. The Christian faith is not simply
about feeling—though feelings are important—but is also
concerned with beliefs and doctrines. So let me speak first
about the content of faith.

Some of the key beliefs we have already touched on
in the previous letter: God is the creator of all things and
made all things good. We are made in God's image and are
called to live life in fellowship with God. We resisted that
call and sin, disobedience, alienation and fragmentation
became part of our lives and our world. God, the redeemer,
in 'his' love reaches out to us in forgiveness, healing and
transformation. God did this particularly through the
life-giving of Jesus, the Son of God. As those impacted
by God's renewing work we are called into communities
of faith for worship, teaching, sacraments, fellowship and
service. We are called to participate in all of life, living to
God's glory and the well-being of our neighbour. In faith
we live to see God's renewing work in our world and await
the final consummation of all things—new heavens and a
new earth.

The *content* of faith is really a summary of the major themes in scripture. This content has been expressed in the creeds, such as the Apostles Creed, and in various confessions and catechisms. I was brought up as a young boy on the Heidelberg Catechism, and the Westminster Confession of Faith was familiar territory for me given my Reformed heritage.

The content of faith is also the province of theologians who have developed various key doctrines. They talk about Christology, the person and work of Christ; Pneumatology, the work of the Holy Spirit; Ecclesiology, the doctrine of the church; Soteriology, the doctrine of redemption; and Eschatology, the doctrine of the Last Things. And these key doctrines are by no means exhaustive.[9] You will remember that in a previous letter I spoke about the importance of belief in the Trinity.

Across the various church denominations these key beliefs and doctrines and the various Creeds are held in common. But there are also important distinctions between Roman Catholicism, Eastern Orthodoxy and Protestantism and then within Protestantism between Reformed, Lutheran, Evangelical and Pentecostalism. For many people this is all very bewildering. They ask, 'How can the one Bible spawn such diversity?' The answer lies not so much in the Bible itself but in the fact that theological traditions have developed at particular periods of history largely as a corrective to what the church had begun to neglect, and these traditions have taken on particular historical and cultural dimensions. Thus diversity lies more with us than with the Bible itself. But more will need to be said about this at a later time. What does need to be said now is that while diversity in unity is healthy, diversity leading to division and competition is a handicap and the curse of denominationalism. Little wonder that people are longing for post-denominational expressions of

Christianity. But more about that when I speak about the church.

So we speak about the *content* of faith. We also speak about *having* faith. Here we are talking about a person's existential experience of trust in God and scripture. So a person may say 'I trust God's promises' or 'I trust the words of the Bible' or 'I trust that God is there and that "he" loves me and all of "his" creation'.

The Reformer Martin Luther made much of the doctrine of justification by faith. This does not mean that *our* faith gives us right relationship with God, but rather that in Christ, God has made possible that we can experience God's friendship, renewal and healing. To know this, to embrace this and to believe this is to have faith and this faith is a gracious gift to us from God 'himself'. This gift is extended to all. God has no favourites. But gifts need to be received and we need to place ourselves open to God's generosity.

Now I believe that content and existential experience must go together. If we only have content then we may know much *about* God, but not know God personally. If, on the other hand, we only have the experience of faith, but no content, then faith may quickly evaporate into feelings.

So what about the matter of doubt, you may ask? Is doubt not the thing that wrecks religious faith? I believe not. It's indifference that wrecks faith. What destroys faith is not the questions we may hurl at God because we feel that 'he' has left us in the lurch. It's not our 'raving and ranting' that does the damage. God can cope with the disappointments that we throw 'his' way. But it is the turning away in cold detachment that begins icing the veins of our soul and narrowing the arteries of our spirituality.

The Psalms express not only the language of faith and trust, but also that of doubt. Psalm 73 struggles with the question of how the wicked can seemingly do so well while the person of faith has nothing but troubles. The writer of this psalm admits that doubt has digressed into creating a bitter spirit. But in working through this doubt, the writer speaks of a renewed faith: 'Whom have I in heaven but you? And earth has nothing I desire besides you. My flesh and heart may fail but God is the strength of my heart and my portion forever' (Ps 73:25-26).

Doubt is writ large on the pages of the Bible. The Hebrew slaves doubted God's ability to deliver them. Abraham doubts God's protective care. Job struggles when life has become so difficult and God is so seemingly far removed. Thomas, the disciple of Jesus, doubts the resurrection. Doubt is part of the journey of faith. Sometimes we doubt God's direction for our lives. At other times we doubt the goodness and care of God. And of course, we may have serious doubts about aspects of the church's teaching or direction.

So how can doubt serve faith? To answer this question I need to back up a little bit and speak about the way in which we may live the Christian life in our kind of world. Now while some Christians may say we can live assuredly and even triumphantly, I would disagree. We can only live the Christian life with difficulty, struggle and vulnerability.

This may surprise you, Naasicaa. You may have expected me to say that we can live the Christian life with great confidence. But I don't see that confidence in the major figures of the Bible, not even in the apostle Paul, who was so sure of his mission to speak about the Christ who had turned his earlier life direction upside down. Paul acknowledges that God's power is made perfect in human weakness (2 Corinthians 12:9).

I think that there are some important reasons why we can only live the Christian life in that kind of vulnerable way. The first is that we live the Christian life in faith, hope and love. These are the fragile commodities of our existence. These qualities are there by the grace of God and are sustained and renewed by the Spirit. Thus so much has to be given and received again and again. Secondly, we do not have God as a predictable entity in our 'back pocket', so to speak. God is faithful in 'his' love for us and the world, but God is wholly mysterious. And God's way with us and the way God reveals 'his' purposes to us cannot be packaged or routinized.

But there is much more. First of all, the church in the West, but thankfully less so in the Third World, has become rationalized. We are not living in a church environment that nourishes the deep sources of faith. Instead, 'churchianity' is very much committed to a whole range of pragmatics. The life of prayer, solitude and meditation that nourishes faith is largely lacking from our religious diet. This has deeply impoverished us. Secondly, we live in a world where God's absence seems to be as evident as 'his' goodness. Our world is marked by difficulty and inequality. And there are no utopias, including religious ones. And finally, we have to acknowledge that in spite of God's goodness and grace in our lives we continue to see the realities of faith dimly and continue to fail in so many ways, particularly in the call to love others in the way we care for ourselves.

So I can't see how we can live the Christian life in any other way than in faith and fragility. So where then does doubt come in? Doubt is part of the human condition. It is a signal of our humanity. We are unsure. We falter. We question and doubt ourselves, others and God. Doubt makes us hesitate. It may make us stop. But our uncertainties can open for us an intermediate space where we have to process things anew. While this intermediate space may lead to the slippery slope of skepticism, it may also lead to renewal and recovery. So I come back to where I was earlier: a faith that has experienced doubt is a faith on the road to maturity.

a personal reflection

I was brought up in a Christian family and regularly attended church. I came to faith outside of these two institutions. That strange beginning tells me something about the way of God, namely, that we cannot put God in a box. The church is not the magic dispenser of God. The church at best can only be a servant of God when God chooses to work in and through it. Moreover, the action of God is not limited to the church. God works through and apart from the church. God will always be far greater than the religious institutions that we create.

In the beginning of the journey of faith I was enamoured with Jesus. I avidly read the gospels. I prayed and I experienced the presence of God in my daily life. I was on some sort of a 'high', almost like being romantically in love for the first time.

But the 'bubble' burst. And in looking back I later realized that it needed to burst. The life of faith is not simply one of feeling nice and safe with Jesus. The life of faith also has to do with risk, courage and service. Being enamoured with Jesus can never be simply for ourselves. Moreover, it's so easy to fall into the trap of thinking that the Christian life is all about good feelings.

It is easy to see this now. But at the time I felt quite abandoned. In fact, I felt God had forsaken me. And doubt set in. All my subsequent attempts to recover this early sense of the closeness of God failed miserably. And so a very different journey began—a journey not unlike an eaglet pushed out of the nest. Or was I merely a sparrow that had fallen out of God's hand, but remained in 'his' heart?

The ensuing journey of faith had everything to do with learning to appreciate and be safe in both the active presence of God and the passive absence of God. Putting it this way probably sounds a bit odd. What I am trying to say is that I had to learn that God is present in 'his' absence.[10] This is just like a person who can know the love and presence of her boyfriend who is presently in the United Kingdom exploring his family roots.

I always have to smile, Naasicaa, when you frown and your eyes flash. I can see a question coming my way. I appreciate the way you puzzle over things and don't settle for trite explanations. So you are right, I do need to explain what I mean by the presence of God, since I have used this phrase a number of times. And yes, it does sound a bit vague, even a bit weird.

Karl Rahner once said that Christians will have to become mystics in our modern world or they will probably cease to be anything.[11] I think he is right. Church dogma or liturgy or church structures in themselves will never be enough to sustain our faith's journey in a deeply secularized society. We have to have some sense that God is present to us. By God's presence I do not necessarily mean experiencing supernatural phenomena like a miracle and only then saying that God is present. Nor do I mean that God's presence can only be experienced in the sanctuary or in specifically religious activities. What I mean instead is an inner awareness that God is with us in the journey of life. This awareness is the fruit of the Spirit who indwells us and accompanies us.

I have experienced God's presence as much in 'secular' employment as I have in Christian 'ministry'. I express the previous sentence this way, but don't believe in the distinction. All of life is to be lived to God's glory and in service to God and others. In fact, sometimes God seemed nearer in the rough and tumble of the workplace than in the quietness of religious sanctuary.

So my faith's journey has already spanned more than forty years. I have no sense that I have arrived anywhere.

The struggle and the joy of faith simply continue. I want to be attentive to God, so I read scripture, pray and meditate. As I have gotten older I meditate more and talk less. I desire to see more of God's presence and rule in our world and so I serve broken people in a needy neighbourhood. And I love to encourage others so I am involved in theological education.

When I was younger and involved in urban mission I believed that we could change the world. Now I believe the most that we can do is small acts of faithfulness. Mother Teresa understood this well.[12] Her order cannot solve the problem of poverty in our world. But she and her sisters can live in a community of love and worship and extend that love to the poorest of the poor.

I began this part of my letter by saying that I came to faith outside of the church. But for faith to grow one can't be a solitary as Dietrich Bonhoeffer has so clearly pointed out.[13] So the whole of my Christian journey has involved being part of the church, intentional Christian communities and para-church organizations. One does need companions on the journey, and faith can only grow in community, worship and service. But more about that later.

the sign and contradiction of the community of faith

letter seven

I have to be honest with you, Naasicaa—this is probably the most emotionally difficult topic for me to talk about. This is not because, like so many others, I have been hurt by the church. The reasons are quite different. I have had such positive experiences of intentional Christian community that church has sometimes paled into insignifcance. The related matter is that I believe that the church should be more of a community and less of an institution. And in working for that kind of transformation, I have often been disappointed and discouraged.

In some ways, I would like to pass over the topic of church because it has become problematic for so many in our contemporary society.[1] But we can't ignore this topic. While it is true that Jesus did not speak much about the church, but mainly proclaimed the Kingdom of God, he nevertheless founded a community of disciples of both men and women. The opening verses of Luke 8 give us a bit of a picture of this community. And out of the mission of Jesus and the outpouring of the Spirit at Pentecost, the early church came into being. It has persisted ever since, in both good times and times of persecution and difficulty. So talk about the church we must. It is part of the Christian story.

the problem of the contemporary church

The church in the Western world is in deep trouble. Over the last couple of centuries, and particularly more recently, it has slipped from being a respected institution to being regarded as a largely irrelevant relic. It is seen by many as a narrow 'club' that has little to say to the pluralistic, cultural and technological world in which we live. And as the Western world increasingly has become more secularized, the church has become more and more marginalized.[2]

But this is not the only difficulty. Not only do those outside of the church generally disregard it, but those within the church are also struggling. In fact, the church has become a revolving door: many more leave by the back door than enter the front door.[3] In many European countries, church buildings have become art galleries and restaurants—there was no longer a community of believers to sustain its spiritual life and structures.

There are many factors that contribute to people within the church experiencing difficulty. One is that members do not feel that the church empowers them for life in the real world. The scriptures are often not made relevant for the house spouse, carpenter, medico, business person, unemployed or politician. Secondly, a dynamic spirituality is often lacking. Church services are often liturgical and mundane affairs, with little sense of God's renewing and healing presence. Thirdly, the church—and by this I do not mean the building, but the people of God—often lacks a sense of connectedness and community. The hour or so of worship once a week can hardly draw people into a sense of solidarity or sharing of a common journey. The other factor, of course, has to do with the busy lives we now lead. Those in employment are spending more time at work than before. Some are at work sixty hours per week. Add to this the pressure to upgrade one's professional life and the fact that both spouses are usually working, and there is little time for much else besides family, housekeeping and some recreation.

However, I think that the problems of the church in the West go much deeper. In response to the Enlightenment, with its emphasis on rationality and its critique of revelation and supernaturalism, the church sought to resist by moving onto the same page. And constant attempts were made to explain and defend Christianity in relation to the scientific mindset of the West. The Christian faith thus became more and more rationalistic. Furthermore, in the hundreds of years of colonialization, the church worked too closely with the colonial masters and was less than sensitive to indigenous cultures. This seriously damaged respect for the church for many people. And finally, the church has been largely unable to accept its post-Christendom condition. What I mean by this is that in earlier centuries, church and society more or less reinforced each other and the church was a powerful force in society. Now the church no longer has this sort of respect and influence, but the church is still trying to function as if the old realities are in place.

Karl Rahner has stressed that the church needs to embrace humbly its marginalized status and once again become the church of the 'little flock'.[4] What he means by this is not that the church should become an inward-looking sect afraid of the 'big bad world', but rather that the church should reinvent itself from the grassroots up in order to become communities of faith and integrity, resisting the powers of this age and living prophetic, counter-cultural lifestyles. But more of that later.

a prophetic beginning

The church is not a building—it is the people of God, those whose friendship with God has been restored and who come together for worship, teaching, formation, fellowship and service. In one sense the church has been there for a long, long time. Since time immemorial there have been people who were friends of God. Throughout the pages of the Old Testament we hear of God's desire that 'his' people should live to glorify God and be a light to the nations. And through Israel, God's welcome was extended to the stranger and sojourner and to the surrounding nations. The Old Testament people of God are the forerunners of the church.

Jesus sought to bring about renewal within the tired Judaism of his day. That the church came into being instead is the sad result of radical attempts at renewal, which have failed to bring about the desired transformation. So often the dysfunctional old persists and fails to embrace the new which seeks to make the old more whole. We also see this same story-line throughout the church's two thousand year history. When the church became tired, lukewarm and dysfunctional, renewal movements were resisted. As a result, we have the long history of sectarian movements— the Montanists, Albigenses and Waldensians. And later the Reformation burst on the scene.

Emil Brunner has pointed out that the vision of the early communities of Christianity was radically anti-institutional.[5] The friends and followers of Jesus inspired by the Spirit formed households of faith. They opened their homes and their lives to one another. They shared a common Eucharist, their goods and resources and shared the charism of the Spirit in building up their life together. The early church father Tertullian stated it well: 'Christians have all things in common, except their wives'.

The modality of these early households of faith had little to do with institutional realities, offices, clergy and structures. They operated much more as extended households. In fact, scholars of Early Christianity, including Edwin Judge, have pointed out that this was the basic structure of the households of faith of the Pauline mission.[6] These households included family, extended family, friends, workers in the household industry and others. What is particularly striking about these communities of faith is their egalitarianism. In a patriarchal culture and in a society with strong divisions, the early churches broke social and cultural boundaries. Women prophesied and played a leadership role in some of the communities. Rich and poor shared a common Eucharist. And most amazing of all, Jews and Gentiles found a common friendship in Christ.

Within three centuries this had all changed. The church as 'little flock' became the church of the Roman Empire. The church as people of God became the church of priest and laity. The church as community became the church as institution. People sharing their charisms were replaced by church offices. Storytelling was replaced by creeds. The common meal of the friends of Jesus became the more formal eucharist. And sadly, at the end of first century, Jews and Gentiles parted ways.

My rereading of church history, Naasicaa, is that these developments are not terribly bad, but sociologically *inevitable*. These more 'solid' structures and realities have helped to preserve the church. Max Weber has a point that charismatic beginnings, while creative, are also most fragile and may disappear over time. The move to routinization is both a form of preservation and stabilization, but also a process of rationalization.[7]

But the very strength of the routinization process is also its obvious weakness. Traditional forms and structures become the dominant realities, and the personalism that lies at the heart of the Christian story disappears, or is severely weakened.

The long story of the church is the persistence of its tradition and its perpetual disturbance by renewal movements. These movements stretch from the Montanists of Early Christianity through to the contemporary recovery of house churches in the First World and the base ecclesial communities in the Third World.[8]

why church?

If being a Christian has to do with being a friend of God, why do we need to think about church? Can't we all just be friends of God and live that friendship out in our families, places of schooling, work and in our neighbourhoods? This is a most attractive idea, particularly in our contemporary Western culture which celebrates individualism. Moreover, many in the West have become deeply sceptical of major institutions, whether that be banks, the International Monetary Fund, governments or church denominations.

It is interesting that Ernst Troeltsch, many decades ago, predicted the growing interest in this way of conceiving church. He saw that people would lose interest in the historic churches, as well as in 'sectarian' Christian groups and end up embracing an individualistic Christo-mysticism.[9] Some of my friends have moved in that direction. Theirs has become a coffee-club Christianity of occasional informal times together with no teaching, formation, accountability or pastoral care.

These are attractive ideas. And as people disappear out of the backdoor of the churches this may well be a growing reality. But I disagree with this direction for two main reasons. The first is that it dynamites one of the most fundamental realities of the Christian faith: 'I believe in the communion of saints'. And secondly, it is, in the final analysis, an accommodation to dominant Western cultural values and fails to resist the powers of this age. Let me explain.

I will start with the last point first. An individualistic Christianity simply reflects and reinforces Western individualism. Now a focus on the individual is good and Christianity has contributed to a recognition of the significance of the individual through its teaching that we are all made in God's image and are people of dignity and worth. The philosophy of Kierkegaard is a philosophy of the individual, but always the individual before God.[10] This is a healthy individualism because it sees the person in relationship.

What is unhealthy is the way in which this emphasis has degenerated into individualism, where the emphasis is on independence instead of interdependence, and self-reliance rather than on community and the inter-connectedness of life. The philosophy of Ayn Rand in her book *Atlas Shrugged* reflects this unhealthy emphasis. A Christianity that buys into these kinds of ideas, or at least into this kind of praxis, offers nothing by way of a countervoice to the trends in our contemporary culture, which have rent the very fabric of social cohesion. In other words, I believe the church should be a counter-community.[11]

But the more basic concern is that this individualism violates the nature of God's redemptive activity in the world. This brings me back to my first point. God builds a people; God does not simply save individuals. Throughout the long biblical story we see that God forms community.

And there are very good reasons for this. Christian community not only exists for the building up, nurturing, care and empowering of God's people. It is also there for the corporate witness it can bring to the world. One individual can reflect only a little of God's manifold wisdom, love and care. A community can do this much more effectively. And such a community that is reflecting reconciliation, the sharing of resources, the welcome of the stranger and service to the world can be a challenge to the dominant values of our culture.

So why church? Dietrich Bonhoeffer reminds us that the Christian cannot be a solitary, even when one may be torn away from the community, as he was during his time in Tegel Prison.[12] The Christian is called into relationship with God and brothers and sisters in Christ, and also to extend this embrace to others.

The church is God's idea. It exists for God's glory. It exists to sustain, nurture and empower God's people. It exists to be a witness and servant to the world. Karl Barth emphasises that the church is to be the continuing prophecy of Jesus Christ.[13]

So let's look at these three elements in turn. First, the invisible and eternal God is committed to visibility. God reveals 'himself' in creation, in 'his' laws, in the prophets, in Jesus Christ, in the work of the Spirit and in the church. The church's task is not so much to defend God or to explain God, but to *reveal* God. Secondly, Christianity is not simply about the religious consciousness of an individual believer. It is much more about God's big story of creating and sustaining a people who will honour 'him' and who will demonstrate their love for God in the practice of love for one another, a love that does not simply impact the religious dimensions of life, but all of life. What I mean here is that to be the people of God means to be called to solidarity, mutuality, caring, service and sharing.

And finally, the church does not exist in and of itself and for itself. The church is sustained by the love of God and the love we have for each other. And part of its existence is to be there for the sake of the world. Let me say a bit more about this.

Some Christians erroneously believe that the church should stay away from the world. They emphasize a holiness that means separation. We can think here of the Exclusive Brethren and the Amish. When you think about this, you soon realize how impossible this is. We still participate in the world even when we try to do so from a distance. And of course, the other problem is that when you chose not to participate, you are in fact committed to supporting the *status quo*. So to put this quite bluntly, this also means condoning the evil and injustice in our world. Not to resist the fallen powers of our world and not to work for social transformation is to support what is. This will not do if indeed we are committed to the values of the Reign of God.

Some evangelicals believe that we should only engage the world for the purposes of witness and evangelism. The task is to save souls from eternal damnation. While I do believe that our task is to share the good news of what God has done in Christ with others, I do not believe that that is our only task. I think that Nicholas Wolterstroff is closer to the mark when he speaks of Christianity being a world-formative religion.[14] He is primarily reflecting the Reformed tradition. The purpose of the people of God is to live for God's glory and kingdom in every sphere of human activity: personal, family, social, national and international. And the community of faith is called to impact every sphere of life with the power of God's redemptive and reconciling love: the arts, economics, education, medical care, politics—the list is endless. In other words, God's good news is for our praying as much as our playing, our sexuality as much as our work for justice, our personal lives as much as for the whole society.

But I think there is much more to the story than this holistic vision of the task and mission of the church. The church has a role in the work of societal transformation. In this, it follows the prophetic work of Christ. But the church also has a healing role. In this, it exercises its priestly ministry. I believe that the church needs to exist on behalf of the world and to make its pain and hopes its own. Jacques Ellul talks about the church standing in an intermediate position, where the movement of the Kingdom of God clashes with the worldliness of the world in its unbelief, independence and pride.[15] But the church's position is much more precarious than that. It lives wholly in both the Kingdom of God and the worldliness of the world. And it is to be there as sorrow bearer, intercessor and witness. Being located in both, the church is both a sign and a countersign. It constantly runs the risk of being so heavenly minded that it is no earthly good, or being so identified with the world that it has become secularized and has become an ineffective witness to God's new creation.

renewal

I have worked for a number of years as a social researcher, looking particularly at how change can be implemented in social welfare organizations. One of the things that one soon discovers is that some organizations are socially healthy while others are quite 'sick'. The other discovery is that organizations are often resistant to significant change. There is no problem with tinkering at the edges, but more profound and necessary change is often resisted because it is too painful.

The church forms no exception to this general observation. It, too, is a very human organization and institution. The church also goes through phases of health and ill health. In saying this, I am not suggesting that the church is exactly the same as a secular or community-based welfare organization. It isn't. The church consciously lives out of the belief that God's Spirit is present in sustaining the community of faith. But at the same time, the church is also a human social construction. We create the church's programmes and structures. So a church can also be spiritually and organizationally healthy or unwell.

When we look at the long history of the Christian church, we see again and again the appearance of movements of renewal which have sought to bring new life to the church. Sometimes the church itself was reinvigorated. At other times, this led to the formation of new churches. Here the Reformation is an example. And at other times, new forms of social organization emerged, such as Monasticism from the fourth century on, and now there are the parachurch organizations of the modern era. This persistence of the old and the radical call of the new has been the dialectic of church history. It is also the general movement of history.

There are a myriad of reasons how and why renewal occurs in the life of the church. The most fundamental is that God preserves the church by 'his' grace and Spirit. The other is that the church finds itself in times of social crisis and difficulty and seeks to respond and reinvent itself. Faith is often revitalized in those circumstances. The other factor, not unrelated to the above, is the persistent beckoning call of the gospels which ever call us to the way of faith that turns our values upside down.[16]

The personal and social vision of the Sermon on the Mount, the example of Jesus in forming a community practising common purse, the radical vision of the Jerusalem church in its practice of mutual care and sharing, and the egalitarianism of the Pauline house churches have beckoned Christians throughout the centuries to live a more radical vision of what it means to be the people of God in the world. From the Desert Fathers and Mothers, the Monastic communities, the Anabaptists, the Moravians and up to the present house churches, intentional Christian communities and the base ecclesial communities of the Third World, Christians have sought to live out the *imitatio Christi* through communities that shared a common life of faith, fellowship and care and which sought to serve and transform the world through ministries of proclamation, prophetic witness, social concern and healing.

I think you know, Naasicaa, that we have attempted to be a small part of this impetus towards church renewal. This came about rather unexpectedly. I was not a minister in a church seeking to bring about changes—it was all very different. I was working as a detached urban youth worker on the streets of South Brisbane, which was then full of pubs, the poor, alcoholics and young people doing illegal drugs.

To get to the point of what could be a very long story, I discovered community not in the church nor in the seminary that I had previously attended, but on the streets amongst homeless young people and alcoholics. There is a powerful lesson in all of this and one that I have been trying to make throughout these letters, namely, that the goodness of God is not restricted to the community of faith. It is also in our streets and amongst people who are disadvantaged.

Now, I do need to qualify the above a little bit. I am not suggesting that the church has no sense of community. It has. But it often lacks depth, because amongst the middle class churches that predominate in the West, we worship as capable and self-sufficient people. We tend to keep our needs and issues pretty much to ourselves. The churches of the poor in the Third World are so very different. There people really need each other. And this is also true of the blighted social reality of our inner city streets. Moreover, I am also not suggesting that I experienced no sense of community at seminary. I did, though not so much in our more formal classes. We often met with other students in our home for discussion and prayer, and there a sense of community had fertile soil in which to grow.

But what I experienced on the streets of South Brisbane amongst the poor so challenged me that I began to re-read the Bible and discovered there the emphasis on personalism, inter-relatedness, mutual care and sharing that lies at the heart of community formation. At that time, we lived with a group of other young people in an old Convent in this run-down part of inner city Brisbane, which more recently has become the prestigious place for the Cultural Centre, Museum, Art Gallery, State Public Library and the famous South Bank. From this Convent we contacted people on the streets, operated a drop-in centre, welcomed street people and drug addicts to our meal table and lived as an intentional Christian community, while hardly being aware that that was what we were. Simply put, we were seeking to practice the hospitality of God with the marginalized in the inner city. And Naasicaa, that is where your mother lived as a young girl.

Our experience of Christian community, later more fully informed by reading about the Anabaptists and the Moravians, became formative for our subsequent experience of what it meant to be church. And so various experimental projects came into being, which took the form of therapeutic Christian communities where we took in young people, particularly those with drug-related problems. Our own home was also set up as an extended household where young people off the streets could live in their journey towards wholeness.[17] As well, an inner city, interdenominational church was formed along community lines. We were a part of that for some fifteen years.

You will remember that in an earlier letter I told you about our living in the East Vancouver neighbourhood. The church of which we are a part also has a commitment to community building. This occurs not only in the life of the church as a whole and through the small groups of which people are a part, but also in the formation of intentional Christian communities providing care for people needing help in working through problems and for political refugees seeking to make a new home in Canada.

You do know something about living in community, Naasicaa. Your experience of living with wider family and friends in North Sydney is a little bit like what I am talking about here. There are of course some important differences, particularly the religious dimension which lies at the heart of Christian community.

a fragile future

Church is the friends of Jesus. Church is the community of faith living in relationship with the Triune God and with each other for the sake of the world. Its fundamental nature is not institutional, but communal and relational. But this is no perfect society. Thomas Merton is right that Christian community is most basically a community of reconciliation and forgiveness.[18] This community is called to be a sign to the world and should not be a contradiction or an offence.

As Dietrich Bonhoeffer has pointed out in his *Life Together*, the experience of community is always a gift of God's goodness. It is never the fruit of our clever organizational building and our psychological group dynamic strategies. And as Jean Vanier has so aptly reminded us in *Community and Growth*, community is the place where we are safe with our woundedness, vulnerabilities and disabilities.[19]

In the light of the above, what of the church in the third millennium? One does not need to be prophetic to see some of the broad brush strokes. The one is that the church in the West is a culturally captive church very much influenced by contemporary management models and with a strong entertainment and psychological flavour.[20] This church is hardly a counter-cultural force, notwithstanding the tremendous amount of good the church is doing in the general social welfare area. This church needs to be converted and needs to reinvent itself. The other is that the church in the Third World is more authentic, virile and sacrificial.[21] I suspect that when the church in the West learns the lesson of humility it may well receive help and encouragement from the church in those parts of the globe.

Furthermore, it is clear that while we can continue to speak of a local church and of national churches, we will increasingly have to become aware of the global church. The church is a global movement. Gone are the days when the movement of the church was from the West to the rest of the globe. And gone are the days when a Euro-centric theology was somehow thought to be sufficient for the rest of the world. It is therefore imperative that the church moves beyond ethnocentrism.[22]

The other major point is that while Christianity may be weak in the West, it is still a major force in the world. More that thirty per cent of the world's population regard themselves as Christians.

But what of the finer points beyond these broad-brush strokes? Well, there are several. The first is that the church will need to discard the ballast it is carrying as a hangover from the Christendom model, where the church as a significant institution took on many of the trappings of power. The church of the future will have to become more anorexic. It will have to recover the essentials of the biblical story and form communities that reflect the heart of Christianity.[23] Secondly, the church as a whole will have to become more biblically and theologically literate. One can't sustain a significant response to our modern world based on a Sunday School faith. We need a theologically astute people of God and this means both clergy and laity. Thirdly, the church will have to play a more formative role in shaping people's faith and spirituality. The disciplines of the spiritual journey, the matters of faith and healing, the journey in prayer and contemplation won't be caught by mere church attendance.[24] And finally, the church is fundamentally missional in nature.[25] It is not a pious club. The church will therefore need to recover its vision to be a signpost of the Kingdom, a sacrament to the world, the place of hospitality for the wounded and broken in our society, and it will need to challenge the idols of our time.

One thing is clear: no one who hasn't experienced the love of Jesus and the presence of the Triune God will want to join the church. While it should be a privilege to be part of the church, it is most frequently a cross we have to bear.

I can remember how in 1973 at the Aquarius Festival at Nimbin in New South Wales, Australia, we set up an intentional Christian community to be of assistance to young people with drug-related problems. Some of our contacts came to faith in Jesus, including Roger and Daphne, two wonderful hippies. I remember saying to them, 'Believing in Jesus is one thing—becoming a part of the church and serving the church will be a much more difficult challenge'.

The young Dietrich Bonhoeffer, as I have mentioned earlier, told his father, then a professor of Psychiatry at the University at Berlin, that he wanted to be a theologian and serve the church. His father was rather disappointed and told his son that the church was not a very good institution, to which Dietrich responded, 'Then I will work to change it'.[26] It would be wonderful if you, too, could make your contribution, Naasicaa!

symbols and countersigns of spirituality

letter eight

When I was your age, Naasicaa, I was about to leave 'secular' work and head for mission work amongst the Aborigines in Western Australia. In looking back on that time, I am disturbed that I had the audacity to believe that I had anything to give to these people. I was still 'wet behind the ears'. On the other hand, it was not wholly of my own choosing. I believed that God had called me. And maybe, that is equally audacious! Does the God of the universe actually give puny individuals a 'word' that radically changes their life's direction? However preposterous that may seem, I believe that to be true.

As you know, I was born in Northern Holland in the province of the Friesian cows. My parents migrated to Australia when I was nine. At the young age of fourteen, I had completed my primary schooling and my father insisted that I go to work to learn a trade. I can still hear my Dad saying: 'That will always stand you in good stead'. He was right. At the time, though, I thought he was totally wrong. And so I entered the Printing and Allied trades as an apprentice, while I really wanted to continue my schooling. To compensate I joined a library near work and foolishly began my reading with Plato's *Republic*.

I loved working in this creative field of printing and publishing and had no thoughts of doing anything else. But then I fell sick. It turned out that I was suffering from lead poisoning, for in those days we were still working with typesetting rather than with computers. While in the hospital, I had a premonition that I would leave the publishing industry and begin work with Aboriginal people. This thought was completely 'out of the blue', but that is what happened.

I share this because it gets us into the topic of spirituality. I was no mystic. The Dutch are pretty sober people and the Reformed Church, of which I was a part at that time, was not known for its religious enthusiasm. The mind was emphasized to the detriment of matters of the heart. And at this time, it was still years before charismatic renewal would impact the major denominations. And yet as a very young Christian, I experienced the strange sense that God was speaking to me and seeking to direct my life.

innate spirituality

I in no way want to give the impression that there was anything special about this experience of mine, as if other people don't have similar experiences. Nor do I wish to suggest that spirituality is unique to Christianity. It is not. All religions promote particular forms of spiritual expression. But even more fundamentally, I believe that *all* people have some form of spirituality.

All people have significant dreams and intuitions that prove to be important. All of us experience a sense of transcendence, when we come in touch with something beyond ourselves, and have a sense of spirit when we are empowered in particular ways. I believe that this is so because we bear the mark of God in the very fabric of our being, and that God's Spirit is at work in the world.

What I am saying is that spirituality is not the sole province of the specifically religious person. So we might think of a monk living a life of prayer and solitude and practicing the liturgical cycle as being a spiritual person and having a deep spirituality, whereas we may regard a person working at the stock exchange as having no spirituality at all.

This kind of categorization is most unhelpful, for the person working at the stock exchange may also be a person of prayer, while the monk may be living his life out of a routine that leaves the heart unaffected. But much more basically, the financial consultant may be seeing his or her work as part of their vocation: working with integrity, serving the wider community and doing this by drawing on creative and intuitive resources within. This is a form of spirituality.

Having worked in a number of 'secular' occupations, I have always been struck by people who are thoughtful, caring, creative and empowering. They may never regard themselves as being religious in any way. Yet the very way in which they live life and conduct themselves in relation to others is a form of spirituality.

There are a number of implications that flow from these barebones remarks. The first is that spirituality is a mark of our humanity and is not to be confined to the more overtly religious dimensions of life. Thus we can speak of a spirituality of everyday life.[1] The contours of this spirituality have to do with the affirmation of life and the expressions of good in our world. Secondly, spirituality is a matter of one's entire lifestyle and not of a segment of life. Therefore it is that which textures and colours all of our activities, our praying and playing, our work and rest and the personal as well as the social dimensions of our existence.

a christian spirituality

Christian spirituality is the way we live life empowered by the Spirit. Christian spirituality is our innate spirituality informed and shaped by the gospel. This means that the Christian faith does not so much give us a spirituality, but restructures and reinvigorates the spirituality we already have. This of course also applies to other dimensions of our life. The Christian faith does not give us the ability to love. We already know how to love in particular ways. But the experience of God's love and grace in our lives helps to deepen our love and provides new sources from which love can spring.

So it is with Christian spirituality. One's relationship of faith and trust in God through the Spirit, one's participation in the community of faith and one's personal spiritual disciplines all become resources for the formation and sustenance of one's spirituality. About this I will have more to say in the latter part of this letter.

But I wish to add at this point that these are not *the only* sources for a Christian spirituality. One's general social context, but also the specificity of one's workplace and one's neighbourhood, may be extra sources for such a spirituality.

While this may not surprise you, Naasicaa, since you are a broad-minded person, there are other readers who may be quite surprised by what I am saying here. This is because they have the idea that Christians operate on the basis that the general society has nothing to offer them. In fact, they believe that Christians live in the world as only wanting to convert the world, but are unwilling to learn or receive anything from others. This is not only how others see many Christians, but also how many Christians see themselves. I obviously don't belong to either camp.

Let me explain why I see things differently. God's good gift to me is not only the community of faith, but also the world with its natural and social resources. Christians are not only my friends and provide input and challenge, but people of no religious faith at all also provide friendship, help and care. Thus both the world of nature and the world of people are resources for spirituality.

But let me qualify this. I do believe that we should resist and seek to overcome the worldliness of the world. What I mean by that are values, forces and systems that promote chaos and death, rather than the good that God intends for creation and humanity. But we are invited to embrace the good that is in our world and see that as a resource for Christian spirituality. Thus, in the words of Reformed theology, we may speak of God's common grace as also formative and significant for our spirituality.

A number of things stand out for me in this regard. I have always loved nature. As a young boy, on most days I spent many hours in fields outside of the town of Franeker in Northern Holland. Nature spoke to me of beauty, life, sustenance and tranquility, even though as a young boy I would not have used such words. Nature, for me, was the visible *hand* of God. It was later, in coming to faith, that I discovered the *heart* of God. This love for nature has persisted. And while I love body surfing, it has always been the mountains of the Lamington Plateau in Southern Queensland that have drawn me. I have gone there for over forty years, not simply to walk and to see its beauty, but to be inwardly renewed and to be with God.[2]

The other thing that stands out for me has been the recognition that at times groups of people or particular social movements reflect values that are closer to the gospel than those being currently practised by the churches. I have already spoken in my previous letter of finding community amongst street people in South Brisbane rather than initially finding it in the church. To this I could add other stories: community-based organizations practising a level of care and empowerment that was far ahead of similar Christian organizations, co-operative movements, just banking. The examples of the practice of good by those who do not see themselves as part of the Christian story are endless. And then we may think of the way in which education, work and the arts have enriched and deepened our lives and brought us closer to the purposes of God.

In the above, I am, of course, speaking about my own experience and my own perspectives. There may be others who are not inspired by nature or by the way that people serve others in the practice of justice. What touches one person's heart and imagination may not deeply affect someone else. What I am saying, though, is that when we live with a sense of openness and reflection, then we can see the hidden hand of God in the rich texture of life. In fact, many have seen the hand of God in places of despair, which has led them to a deeper faith and hope.

sources for christian spirituality

What I have been saying in the above part of my letter is that the sources for a Christian spirituality are not only the reading of scripture, prayer and participation in the community of faith, although these are very important, but also that our connectedness to the earth, our roles in the family, our tasks in the workplace and our participation in the social movements of our time play an important part in shaping our lives. But let me talk about the more traditional sources of Christian spirituality.

Christian spirituality has to do with the way in which we live our lives in God's presence in the midst of the world. It has to do with living every dimension of life—prayer and work, sexuality and politics, creativity and play, relationships and economics and solitude and social engagement—in the light of God's companionship, love and grace.

Spirituality is thus not the pious segment of our lives. It is *the whole of life lived in the Spirit*.[3] Spirituality is, therefore, not simply the practice of the sanctuary, but the outworking of God's love in every dimension of our lives. This, of course, is not to say that the sanctuary is not important in the formation of our spirituality. Nor am I suggesting that the practice of solitude is not important. It is. But so is our work. We can be nurtured, formed and shaped as much by the practice of silence as by our participation in family, work and the general society.

What most fundamentally nurtures and forms our spirituality is the friendship we enjoy with God. The incarnation speaks of God with us, the coming of the Spirit speaks of God within us, and the promise of God is, 'I will never leave you nor forsake you'. To put that only slightly differently, spirituality is living with and being sustained by God's embrace in our lives.

All the sources of Christian spirituality are meant to *mediate* God's presence. The reading of the story of God reminds us of God's passion, ways and promises. It tells us something of who this wonderful God is and the way in which 'he' has acted in history to bring us from chaos to the *shalom* of 'his' Kingdom. Scripture in its stories, history, poetry, prophecy and apocalyptic themes gives us the heartbeat of God. This is God pulling back the curtain of 'his' mystery.

There are a number of ways of reading scripture that can enrich our understanding of the wisdom of God. The first is a general reading for familiarity. It is surprising, but the majority of contemporary Christians have never read the Bible in its entirety. This is all the more surprising since many believe that the Bible is the word of God and should be listened to and obeyed. In my family of origin, we read portions of the Bible each day at meal times and read from Genesis to Revelation. The meal was to nourish us bodily. Scripture was to nourish the soul.

What I was not taught in my family of origin nor in the church that I was a part of was a second form of reading— reading scripture meditatively. This is called *lectio Divina*.[4] Here one might linger with a small passage or even a brief saying and reflect on it. Drink it in. Absorb it, if you like. This practice has long been a part of the Monastic tradition. The value of reading scripture in this way is that a key thought or idea can sink more deeply into the fabric of our lives and become a part of us.

A third way of dealing with scripture is the more academic approach. Here we recognize that the Bible is a very ancient book coming from times and cultures very different to our own. Not recognizing this means that we run the risk of reading our contemporary ideas into scripture. For example, when we see the word 'household' on the pages of the New Testament, we probably think 'nuclear family'. But at that time, a household consisted of family and extended family. It probably also included aunts and uncles, house servants, the workers in cottage-based industry, travelers and visitors.[5] So the conversion of a household to Christ was much more than a private family matter.

The purpose of a scholarly approach allows us to seek to understand the Bible in its ancient cultural settings. It also allows us to look at the Bible more systematically by bringing together all of the prophetic writings, or all of the Pauline letters, or weaving together major themes that occur in the Old Testament and New Testament. Sadly, this approach, while the 'bread and butter' of those studying to become clergy, is sorely lacking amongst the women and men in the pews of our churches. The 'laity', as a consequence, are largely biblically and theologically illiterate.

A further way of reading scripture is a contextual approach. Here we recognize the socio-cultural context in which we find ourselves and identify the strengths and problems of our time. We bring these issues to the scriptures, plumbing this ancient yet ever-relevant book for answers to the questions of our time, circumstances and world.

What I am suggesting is that scripture as a source for spirituality should be engaged in *all* of these ways. We don't just read the Psalms for personal piety. We also read the Prophets for social transformation. In a holistic Christian spirituality we do not wish to disengage the personal from the social. A spirituality of personal piety should have everything to do with the pressing issues of our time, including the gross injustices that continue to characterize our world. After all, the great commandment is to love God *and* our neighbour.

In my previous letter, Naasicaa, I have said quite a bit about the church, the community of faith. I don't want to repeat that here. But I believe that participation in the community of faith is an important resource for spiritual growth and development. I have in mind here participation in worship, teaching, the sacraments and fellowship and sharing. While Cyprian's statement, 'He who hath not the church for his mother, hath not God for his father', is a bit of an overstatement regarding the role of the church, the church is not an optional extra in our spiritual formation.

But here I do not have in mind the contemporary consumer church, where religious professionals provide us with religious services while we remain largely uninvolved and unrelated to one another as members of the church. What I have in mind is church as community where we worship, learn and pray together and where we share life for support and encouragement.

There are also more personal resources for Christian formation: prayer, the practice of solitude, reading the classics of spirituality and engaging in the other Christian disciplines such as fasting and the practice of other forms of asceticism. But more of that later.

a personal reflection

I believe that the initial movement in coming to faith leads to communion. One longs to be with the God of one's discovery in prayer and reflection. This was certainly true of my experience. I avidly read scripture, in particular John's Gospel. I prayed a lot. And I longed to be with God in the comfortability of a newfound friendship grounded in God's love and grace so freely extended towards me. Over time, I began to live my life out of that communion.

But in Protestant and Evangelical churches, emphasis is often placed on another theme: that of service. Spirituality is linked to service and the theme of communion often becomes submerged or neglected. Unfortunately, I was influenced by this kind of thinking. As a result, ministry and mission became more important than fellowship and communion.

This had some disastrous consequences. What I was doing and achieving in urban ministry became at times more important than my friendship with God. And ever since, this has been a great struggle in my Christian journey. I believe that action should come from contemplation.

What we do should emerge out of our friendship with God. But so often this becomes twisted the other way round. We do all these things and then ask God to help us.

I think that P. T. Forsyth has put this in a proper perspective. He writes, 'It is truer to say that we live the Christian life in order to pray, than that we pray in order to live the Christian life'.[6] Or to put that differently, God desires our friendship, not simply our works. But I will say more about prayer and contemplation later.

A further challenge in my own spiritual journey was that I was never prepared in my Christian formation to anticipate and face 'the dark night of the soul'. I was taught that God would always be there in 'his' mercy and love and that I would grow to Christian maturity through participation in the life of the church, personal devotions and service and obedience. I was left with the impression that this would be a smooth and steady journey upwards. I was in for a shock and surprise.

There have been a number of times where I have experienced what I would now call the absent presence of God. At the time, I had no words for this experience and I have been at a point of despair thinking that God had left me. And of course, it had to be my fault! After all, I was far from loving God with my whole being and my neighbour as myself.

I have subsequently learned, particularly through the writings of St John of the Cross, that there are times when God withdraws the active signs of 'his' presence. The wisdom of this is that we learn to trust God not for the good feelings that 'his' presence brings, but that we love God for who 'he' is.[7]

There are related lessons in the journey of faith. The one is that we learn that God does not automatically guard us from the brokenness and madness of our world. In other words, bad things do happen to 'good' people. The other

and related matter is that Christians do participate in
suffering, whether that be their own or that of others.

One of the surprises for me in this area has been the
discovery that at times the suffering of others can impact
us more deeply than our own problems and difficulties.
When the other person, with his or her needs and fragility,
comes to roost in our inner being, we seem to be able to
display an amazing capacity for care and identification.
And for a brief time we 'carry' that person. Rollo May
called this the exercise of nutritive power, which seeks to
give life to the other.[8] Psychologically this is the exercise
of the vicarious dimension of life. In terms of Christian
spirituality, it is receiving a prayer burden and concern for
another that leads us to act on that person's behalf. That
this is temporary and transitional should be obvious. We
can't live long-term with the acute pain of others. And
we can't live indefinitely *for* others. This would lead to
unhealthy dependencies. Thus we have to grow to live *with*
others and to live interdependently.

Throughout my journey of faith I have often thought
about the loneliness of God. In saying this, I in no way
wish to deny that God is a community of persons. Nor
do I wish to suggest that God needs us, in the sense that
God is somehow incomplete without our responsive love
and worship. I believe there is nothing inherently lacking
in God. But I do believe that God has opened 'his' being
to relationship. God's loneliness lies not so much in the
fact that there are not a lot of people who acknowledge
'him'. There are millions, more than thirty percent of the
world's population, in fact! The loneliness lies elsewhere. It
lies, first of all, in the otherness of God and the mystery of
'his' being. We will never fully understand or comprehend
the being of God. Secondly, it lies in the malignment of
God. God has been blamed for it all: wars, repression
of beauty and sexuality, fanaticism, narrow-mindedness,

fundamentalism. This list is endless. In our modern world, Nietzsche has been the great maligner, although a more careful reading suggests that Nietzsche was more frequently upset with Christianity than with Jesus.[9] Thirdly, and for me the most important, the loneliness of God lies not so much is 'his' misunderstoodness, but in his voluntary powerlessness. While I do believe that God is all powerful—after all 'he' called the cosmos into being—in the way that God deals with us, 'he' has chosen the way of vulnerability.[10] God could come to us as commander, but chooses to be lover. God could come to us as demander, but chooses to be giver. 'He' could come as judge, but instead offers forgiveness and grace.

What particularly strikes me about God's vulnerability is that in Christ God has made available redemption and freedom for all, oppressors and the oppressed included, but God in no way forces 'his' blessings upon us.

My prayers, as a result, are not only for myself and others. I have also learned to cry for *God*.

themes for a spirituality

There is much more I could say about my own journey of faith, but the above will give you a bit of a feel of some of my perspectives. In this part of the letter, I would like to say a bit more about some of the important themes for a Christian spirituality. And the best way to come at that is to use a number of important metaphors.

I want to begin with the hospitality of God. Christian spirituality has to do with welcome. It is being welcomed 'home'. This welcome presupposes our lostness and the generous and seeking heart of God. It is a welcome to an embrace and to a table. True hospitality is a welcome to heart and hearth.[11] With the welcome into God's friendship comes the invitation to enjoy God's generosity. And the biblical story is full of words that speak of *shalom* and blessing.

Secondly, Christian spirituality is an exodus spirituality. This has multiple layers of meaning. Its primary meaning is redemptive. God in 'his' grace sets us free from our captivities and idolatries. The social, psychic and spiritual powers that seek to shape and trammel us, leaving us unfree and driven, are subverted by the Spirit's renewing power. We can breathe the fresh air of women and men released from the caverns of our folly and dependencies. The secondary meaning of an exodus spirituality is that having been called out of our captivities, God now calls us from our familiar preoccupations, places and relationships to join with others in their quest for wholeness. In other words, our freedom frees us to serve others. God's redemption is such that it draws us into the purposes of God for the blessing and transformation of our world.[12]

A further metaphor in Christian spirituality is that of the desert. Spirituality is asceticism. I don't mean an asceticism that is seen as the precursor to God's blessing. To put this more bluntly, it is not a spirituality where I deny myself in order to get something from God. It is the other way round. It is having been so greatly blessed by God's generosity that I will say 'no' to things in order to make greater room for God and to serve God's kingdom. Moreover, the desert reminds us of the empty place, the lonely place and the place with no resources.[13] In the spiritual journey we have to learn to live with open and empty hands. We have to learn to come to still places in order to hear our own heart and the heart of God.

One cannot talk about Christian spirituality without talking about prayer and contemplation.[14] Prayer is not beseeching God to wrench things out of an unwilling hand. Prayer is a communion that flows from friendship and fellowship. Prayer is being with God in conversation, and as such, prayer involves talking with God about all of our lives, not only what we need. While prayer has to do with speaking, contemplation has to do with listening and reflection, with being attentive to God. But contemplation also means being attentive to our hearts, others and the heart cry of our world. In this reflective posture we seek to hear and to discern. Thus often contemplation leads to prayer.

I further believe that Christian spirituality is fundamentally relational and communal. It is not a spirituality of the solo hero performing the herculean task. This is not to say that there have not been outstanding leaders in the life of the church—we need only think of St. Augustine, St. Anselm, Teresa of Avila, or more in our time, of Thomas Merton, Mother Teresa, Dietrich Bonhoeffer. Christian spirituality is a spirituality that draws on the biblical witness and the better moments of the history of the church. It is thus a spirituality of the 'communion of saints'. Moreover, this spirituality will always seek to include others and draw them forward. It reaches the hand out to others. It is inclusive and not exclusive.

In my various other letters to you, Naasicaa, I have touched on the fact that I believe Christian spirituality to be rooted in everyday life. While some older Christian spiritualities are very esoteric, I believe that Christian spirituality is more a bread and butter spirituality. Perhaps this idea turns you off? By this I do not mean that it is mundane and boring, nor am I denying that it is transcendent and mysterious, belonging to the Spirit world. But I do mean that it has to do with life here and now and not simply with the life to come. I don't believe that we should live the Christian life in order to go to heaven. I believe, instead, that we should live life as if heaven is already partly present. This spirituality, therefore, is not only for the monk or priest. It is for the ordinary person: the student, the motor mechanic, the politician. It is a spirituality that encourages us to think about our relationships, work and leisure—every dimension of life.

This means that this spirituality is holistic. It does not segment off one area of life. It encourages us to think about our motivations, choices, occupations, relationships and our life's orientation. It sees life as interconnected. My life with God has something to do with my relationships with the neighbour. Prayer has something to do with politics.

Finally, Christian spirituality is eschatological. What I mean by that is not simply that it looks forward to the world to come, though this is part of it. We do not simply live for now, but also for God's final future. But what I also have in mind is that this spirituality has to do with the present work of God's Spirit in our lives, in the church and in history. The Spirit opens us to the world of dreams, the wisdom of intuition, the gift of discernment, the reality of healing. The charisms of the Spirit are the pinpricks of God's final future. These gifts of the Spirit enrich our lives. They carry us beyond the rational into the mysterious workings of God.[15]

countersigns

I have spoken about the symbols of Christian spirituality in the section on themes and metaphors. This section, of course, was by no means exhaustive. And we could use other symbols: that of bread and wine in the Eucharist, water in baptism, the dove in the coming of the Spirit. The language of the Bible is rich with images expressing the way God works in our lives, the church and the world.

But what do I mean by countersigns? Simply put, I believe that there are spiritualities that are not the conveyors of life, but of death. And the place to focus, first of all, is not on the outside world, but within the church itself.

Subtle counter spiritualities can occur when the church has become unhealthy and is no longer empowered by God's Spirit. The most basic forms of counter spiritualities I have in mind are legalism, rationalism, misuse of institutional power and the personality cult.[16] While all of these are equally dysfunctional, the misuse of power is often the most serious, because it is claimed to be exercised in the name of God. It is always amazing to me how the most enthusiastic groups of Christians often take on 'cultic' overtones because they have failed to convert the power of control into the power of servanthood.

Your mother would have told you, Naasicaa, that in the late 1960s through to the 1980s we worked with young people in the drug scene. Many of these young people had explored various esoteric religions, had sat at the feet of various gurus, had ingested hallucinogenic substances and had dabbled in various forms of occultism. None of this was particularly impressive. In fact, for the majority, this dabbling had been downright dysfunctional and dangerous.

You are frowning again, Naasicaa. And rightly so! You think what I am saying is too negative, even judgmental, perhaps? This dysfunctionality could simply have been the problem of the young people themselves, rather than the religious systems they were exploring. And the problem could have been the drug concoctions they were taking. In other words, if they had embraced Buddhist spirituality, for example, they would have reflected the signs of life, rather than the contours of death.

I agree. There are life-giving spiritualities other than the Christian one. So what then should one look for in a spirituality and what should one avoid? Let's start with the latter.

A spirituality is death-dealing if it fragments major dimensions of one's life. For example, it might have answers for one's peace of mind but not for one's body, relationships and place in the world. Secondly, it might be fundamentally narcissistic. In other words, it might only have the 'me' in view in terms of self-realization and self-enhancement, but fails to have a heart for others. Thirdly, it is death-dealing if it is elitist. So appealing but so dangerous are the groups that claim to have the only inside information and the only ladder to the esoteric world. Fourthly, a spirituality is unhealthy if it is isolationist. What I mean here is that it might sever friendships, family networks and one's connectedness with the wider world.

There are, however, other signs of death. The most basic is a spirituality offering self-enhancement through self effort with no redemptive dimension. There is no recognition of our own sinfulness and folly and no empowerment for our inner transformation.

This brings me to what we should look for in a spirituality. It must empower me in all the dimensions of life—my relationships, my inner well-being, my relatedness to the world. It needs to provide answers for the negative powers at work in my life and for my own brokenness. It needs to be defensible in general discourse. I can't just say this is my own thing without being able to talk about it and open it to scrutiny and discussion. Spirituality may be personal, but it is not secretive.

The above are some bottom-line issues. You need to know, Naasicaa, that I am quite sensitive to the way in which we can open our lives to the spirit world. This world I believe to be as real as the world of technology. It is a world that can enrich us, but it can also bring us into bondage. Over the years, I have had to perform exorcisms with people who opened their lives to powers which they thought were beneficial, but were in fact malevolent.[17]

In doing a lot of thinking about all of this over the years, I have come to a simple conclusion. Because the spirit world is like entering a dark tunnel in which you don't know beforehand whether it leads to an oasis or a desert, light or further darkness, freedom or bondage, it is important to have a guide and it's important to know this guide. If the guide is a self-indulgent guru living a life of luxury gained from the adoring faithful, then I have serious doubts about this guide and where he or she may wish to lead me.

This is why I have put my hopes on Jesus as my guide to the world of the spirit. His life of love, compassion, wisdom, service to the poor and healing is a powerful sign that he can lead me to the spirit world of the Good Spirit. In fact, Jesus promises that he will pour out the Holy Spirit upon us. But more about that in another letter.

I have reread parts of this letter while back in the Philippines. I am teaching a module course at Asian Theological Seminary, where I taught full-time for six years in the early 1990s. It strikes me how the world of the spirit is much more familiar to Asians and also others in the Third World, but less familiar to us in the First World. The West has long been subject to a period of rationalism and rationalization, which has made the world mundane and devoid of awe and wonder. Mystery has been strangled by so-called scientific predictability and the spirit world has become a strange domain for us. Although there are many signs of hope, post-modern Westerners are exploring more open, intuitive and integrative approaches to life.

We have much to learn and unlearn. What I find interesting is that the Bible is not a Western book. It is 'Asian'. Maybe in the future it will be Asians, or others from the Third World, who will teach us about prayer, meditation, the supernatural, and the realm of the Good Spirit—the Spirit of God.

a concluding comment

The heart of spirituality has little to do with certain religious practices championed by the respective religious traditions. The heart lies elsewhere. True spirituality is to live a life of love that comes from being loved in God's embrace. It is this embrace that empowers us in the journey to wholeness and frees us to love others. In the words of St Augustine, love is the movement from *cupiditas* to *caritas*, from self-centered love to other-centred love.

This same church father made the further observation, 'When there is a question as to whether a man (or woman) is good, one does not ask what he (or she) believes . . . or hopes, but what he (or she) loves'. And it is this observation that leads to the heart of the gospel: to love God and our neighbour as ourselves.

Christian spirituality is the following of Jesus empowered by the Spirit. Its contours are love, forgiveness and peacemaking. It seeks to honour God and to serve the world. There is nothing easy about this kind of spirituality. It is not a Saturday picnic. Rather, it is a life marked by the cross of Christ.

themes of life and threads of decay

letter nine

After all these years I still feel sad about the fact that I was only able to attend the birth of my last born daughter, your Aunty Jodie. The hospital system in Australia in the 1960s did not allow fathers to be present. We were supposed to go fishing! After all, babies were regarded to be woman's work. No matter how much we pled with the doctors, the answer was always 'no'. During Rita's pregnancy with Jodie, hospital policy finally changed.

It was an awesome experience to see Jodie burst into the world. Joy in the midst of pain, body fluid and blood. I was stunned for days afterwards and remember penning several poems lauding the gift of life.

While I have been back in Brisbane, I have been visiting my mother who has been sliding towards death for several years. She is in her late eighties and suffers from dementia. She no longer recognizes me when I visit and can no longer speak.

Life is the span of the joy of birth and the inevitability of death. Francois Mitterand once commented that 'birth and death are the two wings of time'. And in between these two points of a beginning and an end, we have a lot of living to do. This living is increasingly longer in the First World due to better nutrition and health care.

My grandfather lived to be ninety-six. Rita's mother is already ninety-three. So Naasicaa, there are some pretty strong genes that have been passed on to you. You may live a long life! But of this we can't be sure, can we? Life is finally not in our control.

If you think that in this letter I am going to give you ten steps to live a happy and fulfilled life (some want to add prosperous as well) you can relax. I think that most of this kind of advice promoted in popular books and magazines is a lot of superficial nonsense. As if there are simple steps to live the greatest mystery—life itself! As if we can make it all happen! As if we are in control of all that may occur in our lifetime! Moreover, the happy life seldom occurs through seeking happiness. It more frequently happens in ways that we had never expected or anticipated.

So you won't get a ten-step program from me. Furthermore, I can't really tell you how you should live *your* life. Hard as it may sound, you have to find your own way. In other words, you have to sort out the way in which you wish to live. You have to make choices. You have to set your sails in a particular direction. But you need not do this on your own. There are many who love you and are committed to you and who want to see you grow and develop into a person of purpose.

know thyself

The above phrase is a famous ancient Greek saying that sees self-understanding as being intrinsic to wisdom. It also has everything to do with what we are considering here—what is life-giving. And of course, one can't consider that without also asking the question—what is death-dealing? This set of ideas, asking what is life-giving and death-dealing, comes from Ignatian spirituality.[1] Thinking in this way has been most helpful to me as I have had to make important life choices. But more about that at some other time.

Now the question is probably rumbling around in your head: How can knowing myself have anything to do with what is life-giving? Let me get to the point. There are two elements at work here. The first is that I need to live life within the framework and possibilities of who I am and how I am gifted. The other is that I cannot live someone else's dream for my life, whether that someone be an especially important person, or whether these are the corporate dictates of a society.

To 'know thyself' has to do with self-understanding. And in the journey of understanding ourselves, a lot of mystery has to be revealed. In the words of Martin Heidegger, a lot of unveiling needs to take place.[2] Put differently, I need to get to know my own being, as well as my potential. I need insight into who I am, as well as the courage to become who I want to and should be.

This double movement is the exciting promise facing every young person. I need to know increasingly how I 'tick', or better put, how I operate in the way I think, process things, plan, communicate, do things and how I relate to others. This becomes clearer over time through self-insight and through the feedback that others give us. This also becomes clearer through the clashes we have with others and through difficulty.

Along with this, I need to become more and more
aware of what gifts have come my way through my genetic
inheritance and how significant others have been able
to encourage me and bring out some of my abilities. It is
amazing that we have been so richly endowed and that
so many talents, like uncut diamonds, lie within the dark
caverns of our being.

Here the life of faith also plays a crucial part. To know
myself in the light of God's love and to appreciate the way
in which God has made me and gifted me is essential to my
self-understanding. Moreover, the gift of the Holy Spirit,
as the Spirit of truth, plays an important part in coming to
self-insight.

But this spiritual dynamic can also be complemented
by other means and there is no reason why psychological
or vocational testing should not be helpful. I have found
both the Myers-Briggs[3] and the Enneagram[4] to be helpful
in later life, but I see these as *mere indicators* and not as
descriptions of who I am. We are all far more complex than
any test can indicate.

Along with growing in understanding regarding my
gifts, talents and orientation comes the complimentary
dynamic of understanding my limitations. This is not the
signal to a passive resignation. Nor does this undermine
finding the courage to become who I want to be.[5] It is
simply the ability to face the sober reality that I am not and
cannot be anything and everything. If my gifts, choices and
opportunities move me to become a ballet dancer, then I
cannot also become a heavyweight lifter.

Most of us struggle with accepting personal limitation.
We somehow think that we can be and do anything and
everything. But that is impossible. We are not God and
fundamentally not even godlike. At this point, contemporary
society and its values do not serve us well. We are given
the idea that everything is available to us and that we can

do anything and be everything, providing we have the financial resources. This is a myth.

H-G. Gadamer has rightly pointed out that every time we say 'yes' to one thing we are by implication saying 'no' to something else.[6] And, Naasicaa, I think that you have already felt the pain of this. This pain operates at several levels. One level of pain is coming to terms with the illusions we have about ourselves in thinking we can be and do more than we in fact can. At another level, we are 'forced' to make choices. One usually can't do law and engineering at the same time. And one can't marry two men at the same time, at least not in our culture!

Rather than seeing limitation as a curse, we may see it as a gift. For by having to make choices and having to say 'yes' to one direction and 'no' to another, we have the opportunity to find a sense of direction, to discover our calling and to consolidate aspects of our lives.

I talked earlier about this double movement. The one is gaining insight into who I am. The other is grasping the courage to become who I want to be. I now need to say some things about the latter. Within the broader limits of my humanity, giftedness and the general circumstances of my life, there is an openness. I can do and become a number of things. I can make vocational and relational choices. I can make decisions about my lifestyle. And all of these things have to do with the person I am becoming. Thus I have not only been given much in terms of who I am, but I also play a part in becoming the person I wish to be.

About this exciting journey, let me say a number of things. One, in making choices, we need wisdom and discernment. In gaining that, I believe we need the guidance of God's Spirit, we need to listen to our heart as well as our mind, and we need to be open to the advice of others. Secondly, we need the courage to live our choices and to take responsibility for our lives. Alongside that, we need to grow in humility, realizing that some choices may not have been helpful. Life is not about always getting things right, but moving in the right direction after we recognize that we have made mistakes. E. Stanley Jones, a friend of Gandhi, once said, 'If I fail, I want to fail in the right direction'.

If I had to summarize in different words what I have said in this part of my letter to you, I would say the following: it is life-giving to live according to one's giftedness and abilities; it is hard to live life against itself. Unlike my father and my two brothers, I had no gifts, abilities and inclinations to work in trades that required mechanical know-how. If I touched a machine, it usually broke down. And in the years that I worked in the Department of Social Work and Social Policy at The University of Queensland, I was banned from using the latest photocopier for that very reason.

Not to live within the framework of one's giftedness and abilities is to weave one's life with the threads of decay and death. One can't continue to attempt to be what one is not. While this attempt may come from one's own illusions, it more frequently comes from the pressure and expectations of others. Thus to be oneself involves resisting the dreams of others. It requires the courage to be oneself.

knowing others

As in all the letters I am writing to you, Naasicaa, I am not being exhaustive in my coverage of topics, but only suggestive. This is also true of the above section. There is much more I could say, including that in learning to know ourselves we also need to face the dark side of ourselves. But I will talk about this at another time.

Here I want to talk about relationships, about knowing, being known and knowing others. Knowing others, particularly in the fragile and challenging art of friendship, has much to do with knowing ourselves. We need to know who we are and what we can share and give in our relationships with others. This, of course, is not to deny that in deeper friendships we not only share our knowability, but also our mystery.

In friendship, we not only learn to know others, but we ourselves need to be known by others. In other words, we need to take risks in vulnerability and openness. Thus reciprocity and mutuality are key dimensions in the journey of friendship. It is important to realize that this is not true of all relationships. In seeing a psychiatrist, for example, the dynamic is quite different. He or she seeks to know us in our strengths and psychopathology. But it is unlikely that we will get to know the psychiatrist.

This example raises an important issue in relationships, namely, the matter of power. In a relationship of helper and helpee the dynamic of power is not equally distributed. The former has more power than the latter, although the helpee is far from powerless. He or she can refuse to heed the advice and reject the help of the helper.

It is important, Naasicaa, that you think through this issue, for it has ramifications like the tenacles of an octopus. In ordinary relationships, a healthy experience of power is to have power *with* others. But there are always people who want to have power *over* others in a way that is not to the other's benefit. A healthy way to have power *over* others is to have a willingness for others to participate in that power for themselves, or in other words, for them to be empowered. What I have in mind here is the more knowledgeable or the more skilful person sharing their gifts and abilities in ways that facilitate growth in others. This results in power *with* others. What is unhealthy is when gifts or abilities are used to manipulate others or to make them dependent.[7]

We need to be aware when others exercise power over us in unhealthy ways and equally careful that we don't exercise that kind of power in relation to others. We need to exercise power over ourselves in order to relate in appropriate ways to others.

All of this, of course, is related to the much broader issue of hierarchies that exist in social life. We have the rulers and the ruled, the boss and the employee, the clergy and the laity and not so long ago we thought of the husband and wife in hierarchical terms. Not only is the last named no longer understood as a hierarchy but as a relationship of mutuality, so also in other areas of relationship and work there has come a flattening of the power differentials. Workers also have power. So have the laity in the church. What is particularly important is that these hierarchies do not operate in our relationships of friendship.

That relationships can be life-giving is self-evident. But let's talk about it anyway. Apart from the relationships of family and extended family, which are a given, most other relationships are of our own making. This does need some qualification, however. We don't choose our teachers, fellow employees, church members and neighbours. Some of these may never become friends. Some, in fact, may be a nuisance factor in our lives. But most of our adult relationships are the ones we choose to develop.

This development is always a movement from stranger to potential friend, from acquaintance to close friend and from friend to possible life partner. This movement requires an interesting dialectic between maintaining our own boundaries and being open to the other. It involves risk taking as well as growth in trust. It involves the movement of giving and receiving. Above all, it needs to be a relationship of freedom and mutuality and not of manipulation and dependency.

Healthy friendships are not only a source of companionship, care and encouragement. They are also a source of revelation. What I mean by this is that in life-giving friendship, we come to understand ourselves better. We discover more of how we think and operate. We also come to see some of our blind spots in the face of the other.

You have met some of our friends, Naasicaa and therefore you know how blessed Rita and I are. Most of these friendships were formed during our years working with Teen Challenge in reaching out to homeless youth and drug dependent young people. These friendships were forged in the communities we formed to help these young people in their journey to wholeness. These friendships are still strong today, even though we have been away from Australia for over fifteen years, and we have all gone into other areas of work and ministry. I regard these friendships as a most precious treasure.

In this, I see some important elements for friendship building. Even though I use this kind of terminology, I still believe that friendship is fundamentally a gift. But gifts can be handled in constructive ways. The first element is that friendship can grow when we have the opportunity to see each other regularly and in a diversity of activities. Secondly, friendship can grow when there are common interests and purposes. Thirdly, friendship deepens when we can go through difficulties and hard times together. And finally, friendship cannot be built when we only reveal our strengths. We also have to show our fears and weaknesses.

I wish, Naasicaa, that I could help you find the love of your life. But that is not possible. For this, I can only pray. I certainly don't believe that there is a Mister Right out there for you, nor that marriages are made in heaven. The art of finding someone with whom you fully want to share your life is fraught with difficulty and promise. While love at first sight is always a possibility, but hardly ever the norm, I believe that the movement from friendship to deeper love is a gradual journey. And as trust deepens and love grows, there comes the possibility for more profound commitments.

forgiveness and relinquishment

Using the themes 'life-giving' and 'death-dealing' in the area of relationships, it is obvious that having good friendships empowers us, while being in unhelpful, dysfunctional or destructive relationships weaves the threads of decay. Sadly, relationships with others can be hurtful due to manipulation, neglect or abuse.

While there may be some people who go through life relatively unscathed, and while there may be some who lead 'charmed' lives, that is not the experience of most of us. We both hurt others and are hurt ourselves by the unhelpful things that people say and do to us. And since life is not fair, there is no point in trying to keep a moral ledger. The logic that if I am kind to others they in turn will be kind to me frequently breaks down. In fact, a person that one has loved most deeply may in turn become most cruel. After all, Jesus was crucified by people whom he blessed, not abused.

So if there is anything we can be sure about, it is that we will be hurt in some of our relationships. And of course, the more significant the relationship, the greater the possible hurt and wounding. For some, these hurtful relationships go all the way back to their family of origin. For others, these took place during the more vulnerable years of schooling. For others again, relational hurt occurred in their adult years.

Unless we are very sensitive and intuitive, or unless we have a very strong sense of personal boundaries, we often come to relational difficulties in ambiguous ways. Or we may come to them much too late. What I mean by this is that we often blame ourselves for the neglect or abuse of others because we are never wholly morally free. Moreover, we often allow bad things to drag on in the hope that with time things will get better. They seldom do get better!

What I am saying here is not that we should cut others off the moment difficulties appear in the relationship. If we were to do that, none of our relationships would grow to any depth. But what I am saying is that we should not carry and blame ourselves for the wrong 'stuff' that others put on us. Nor should we remain in abusive relationships because we have developed some co-dependency.

The fact that we are hurt by the sins of others against us and that we also sin against other people opens up for us the challenging art of seeking and extending forgiveness. C.S. Lewis, whose Narnia series you avidly read when you were younger, reminds us in many of his other writings that the most basic movement towards life is the movement to forgive.[8] Forgiveness is the bread and butter of human existence.

I believe that if we have hurt and emotionally wounded others, then we need to apologize and seek forgiveness. If others have hurt us, then I believe we should forgive whether they apologize or not. Obeying the divine impulse to forgive is both life-giving for us and for the one who has hurt us.

Forgiving those who have hurt us is not usually our first thought. We want to retaliate and also hurt him or her in some way, even if it is through avoidance and subsequent neglect. But when forgiveness is our second and final thought, it is a mark of grace and is spawned by love.

Forgiveness lies at the heart of the gospel. God's redemptive love is for a humanity that rejects or ignores 'his' love. Forgiveness is also the fruit that the difficulties in our relationships may produce. The Russian author Alexander Solzhenitsyn had to find this grace for those who put him and kept him in the Gulag.[9]

While the dynamic of forgiveness in relationships is mysterious enough, the matter of relinquishment is even more mysterious. Relinquishment involves the voluntary handing over or letting go of something that is rightly ours. Now you may be wondering, Naasicaa, why I am wanting to talk about this as a theme of life. Is it not rather a theme of death? Well, in one sense it is, for it may involve dying to something. But this dying gives life. These are not the threads of decay.

Relinquishment is not the favourite topic in our contemporary Western culture. In fact, our culture's theme is the opposite—much-having. Ours is a consumer culture in which having is important to self-enhancement—the more expensive the better. So implicitly, our culture is telling us that much-having equals happiness and well-being. Not to have something is to be deprived and to be less than what one could or should be.

This emphasis in our culture is grossly lopsided, for well-being does not rotate simply around having, but also around relinquishment. At its motivational centre, this is the ability, in the words of Henri Nouwen, to live life with open hands.[10] It is also a form of self-giving and possibly, even more profoundly, the willingness to bend to the mystery of life by releasing that which we feel we should not cling to.

The more natural impulse is to live life with a closed fist. I do not mean that we are shaking that fist in someone's face with the threat to violence. I simply mean that we want to hold tightly to what is ours. And however understandable that may be, there are several problems in living this way. The first is that we may squeeze to death what we are holding. We can cling to something so much that it becomes the core of who we are and as such it becomes idolatrous. Secondly, the closed fist never leaves our hand open and empty. We are in control, but there is no room for surprises. And thirdly, not to be able to let go means that we will never know the blessedness of the movement from death to life.

Whether we like it or not, things will be taken away from us. People will disappear out of our life. The company we work for may fold. And the later aging process, in the words of Scott Peck, is a fearful stripping process.[11] Relinquishment is not what is taken from us. It is what we are willing to let go of.

Thus strange as it may seem, having full hands is not life-giving. Our hands sometimes need to be empty so that new things may come to us.

a closing reflection

As I have told you in an earlier letter, we moved from the better side of Vancouver to a more run-down East Vancouver neighbourhood. Some saw that as some sort of a sacrifice. It wasn't. We gained much more by living in that community than we did in our isolation in suburbia. Moreover, by joining Grandview Calvary Baptist Church, a community church committed to holistic ministry, we had the joy of being part of a larger group that had a similar vision to our own.

What is life-giving cannot simply revolve around ourselves. To be part of a movement or organization that champions values similar to our own is very empowering. That is why, for the Christian, the challenge to be part of God's purposes for the world is very life-giving. What I mean by this is that in gaining a sense of what God would have us do with our lives in terms of our work and service in the world, our lives take on a fuller meaning.

This is no narrow vision. And serving God's purposes does not simply mean becoming clergy. One can serve God as an artist, scientist or educator.

I have written about some themes of life. By this I am not proposing some upbeat version of life, a life with a full wind in the sails—as if there are no doldrums and no storms! Life is not that smooth. The threads of decay are always with us. And life knows both joys and sorrows. But it does matter what we lean towards. For you, I trust that it will always be in the direction of what is good and life-giving.

I am finishing this letter while in Yangon. I have just spent time with some of my Burmese friends working in a very difficult section of the city. They have little in the way of infrastructure and material resources and yet somehow their life is full. They have vision. They are blessing the community in which they live. They have a sense that God is with them and is sustaining them.

They are a living reminder of what I have been writing about in my letter to you. Emptiness can be the seedbed of life. Relinquishment can be a blessing in disguise.

passion, commitment and disillusionment

letter ten

The first time I arrived at Yangon airport in Myanmar some years ago, I was shocked. Here was a military regime at loggerheads with Western democracy and resistant to the pressure of the international community calling for the restoration of human rights. I had expected, therefore, that the airport foyer would be adorned with the symbols of Burmese culture in its defiance of the West. But this was not the case. I was met by the illumined signs of Western consumer products. I was most disappointed.

I share this observation not because I support the Burmese regime. Nor am I in principle opposed to Western consumer products. I live with the benefits that such products bring. Nor am I opposed to the amazing network of world trade that allows one to buy one's favourite products virtually anywhere in the world, including in the poverty stricken Third World. But I am concerned about some of the bigger issues that lie at the back of this, including the cultural globalization of our world.

Saying that I am concerned about this leads me to point out that I am also concerned about many other related issues. I am deeply concerned about the poverty of the Third World. I find it perverse that rich countries with only fifteen percent of the world's population control eighty percent of the world's wealth. This leaves middle and lower income countries with eighty-five percent of the world's population holding only twenty percent of the world's wealth. What is the most depressing is that nearly sixty percent of the world's population live in poor countries that have only five percent of the world's total income.

What lies embedded in these huge disparities between the First World and the Third World is not simply a lack of equality, but a lack of justice. There is ongoing systemic exploitation occurring in our world. The West's exploitation during the former colonial period is far from over. The colonies may be no more, but the exploitation continues through trade arrangements, the financial indebtedness of the Third World to First World financial institutions and the cultural and economic imperialism of the West. In saying this, I am not implying that the Third World has the high moral ground and is 'squeaky' clean. It has its share of oppressors and corruption. But I am saying that the West is morally culpable. There is nothing distinctly Christian in its role in the world. It only knows how to take. Forgiveness, including debt forgiveness, serving the vulnerable poor, empowering the weak, advocating on behalf of the two billion who stare hunger in the face each day and whose faces reflect our neglect—these are not the driving concerns of the West.

passion: its power and weaknesses

Saying that I am deeply concerned about these matters is another way of saying that I feel passionately about these things. While passion means to have a strong emotion about something or to have an intense enthusiasm, its more basic meaning from the Latin *patic* means to suffer. To be passionate is not to be detached, but to be engaged. One is not passionate about something to which one gives scant attention. To be passionate means that one is drawn in, one participates, even to the point of pain.

My concern in writing to you about this, Naasicaa, is that I believe that we are living in a passionless age. And in this, we are experiencing a great loss that affects our humanity and our solidarity in community. To be passionless not only condemns us to support the *status quo*—it also diminishes our humanity. As human beings our destiny does not lie in our meanderings, but in our passions. What I mean by this is that we are meant to feel deeply about things and not to live with the numbness of acceptance or indifference.

I believe that passion is inherent in what it means to be made in God's image and to be God's vice-regents in the world. God did not call the world into being with solemn detachment. God called into being all that is with the passion of 'his' love. Similarly, 'his' passion for justice heard the cry of the slaves in Egypt and God's passion for covenant-keeping brought forth the plaintive cry and the heralding call of the prophets. And it was the passion (note that word again) of Christ, his death on our behalf, that opened the floodgates for God's fuller redemptive activity in our world.

There is nothing calm about God. God is not 'cool' in the sense of a self-satisfied detachment. The God of the Bible weeps and cries. God loves and suffers. God enters

our pain and seeks our transformation. Just listen to Hosea:
'How can I hand you over, Israel . . . my heart is changed
within me, all my compassion is aroused' (11:8). Or, in the
words of Isaiah, 'For a long time I have kept silent, I have
been quiet and held myself back. But now, like a woman
in childbirth, I cry out, I gasp and pant . . . I will turn the
darkness into light before them and make the rough places
smooth' (42:14,16).

In a similar way, we are not to be passionless creatures.
Rather, we are called to enter the passion of God for our
world and for its renewal and transformation. Made in
God's image, we are to reflect the heart of God. And made
for each other, we are challenged to enter the sufferings of
others.

Sadly, our contemporary culture does not encourage
this kind of passion. While our society encourages us to
be passionate about our sexuality, it does not foster passion
about our spirituality and social concern. That sounds too
much like fanaticism. We are, therefore, encouraged to be
rational and, above all, sensible. And ultimately we seek
to be 'cool' with a calm superiority of indifference—these
things won't occupy my inner world!

It is most unfortunate that many of our universities are
now cradles for professional development and not places
for critical thought.[1] And while we may be encouraged
to be skilful and thoughtful within our field of so-called
expertise, we are not formed to be passionate. Become a
sociologist, by all means, but not one who is committed to
the implications of what one teaches and believes! By all
means teach courses on urban justice, but allow me to live
on my rural acreage far away from the pain in the inner
city!

Sadly, the contemporary church is of little help in these
matters. It is happy to speak about the passion of Christ
on our behalf, but has little to say about our passionate

commitments. This should not surprise us, for the church is a highly compromised institution. It has suppressed the dangerous memories of early Christianity. It preaches about heaven, but follows some of the ways of the world. Its life is not marked by the cross, even though its lips are.[2]

One would have expected the Pentecostals to be different. They are known for their enthusiasm. And that means to be filled with the passion of God. But while the early Pentecostals with their Black roots were passionate about the power of God in their midst and equally passionate about mercy and justice, the middle-class, white co-option of the movement led these passions into respectability and eventual mediocrity.[3]

I have been saying that to be fully human is to live with passion, rather than with a bland mediocrity. Passion is at a premium in our Western world. That should not surprise us. The large market forces in our world want people who consume and who augment and strengthen the system. It does not welcome those who come to disturb. And that is what passion does. Thus our world wants the priest, not the prophet.

To live passionately is to live against the central tenets of our contemporary culture.[4] Yet our consumer culture conditions us to live for ourselves. It also conditions us to live safely. These two ideas are interrelated. If we want to enhance ourselves, we need to make ourselves more secure. Since the terrorist attack on the World Trade Centre in New York, our world has become more fearful, and the matter of security has been raised to optimum levels. To live passionately is to take risks and to enter another's issues and pain.

I am not surprised that you may have objections to what I am saying, Naasicaa. All of this sounds too masochistic. Why live this way, if one can avoid it? Why cannot one live for happiness, safety and security? Why should one be passionately concerned about the issues in our world and the questions of our time? And why should one be concerned for others, including one's enemies?

Let me respond even if it involves some repetition. First, to be human means to be passionate. We know how to feel deeply and identify with another's issues and concerns. We also know that we should not really stand idly by when we can contribute to the good. Secondly, God is passionate about the good—so passionate that God in Christ embraced a cruel death to show that a way other than violence is the way to life. We are invited to share and participate in the passion of God by extending forgiveness, being a healing presence in our community and resisting the oppressive powers that scar our world—including those of materialism and greed, ethnocentrism and racial hatred, militarism and exploitation.

Without passion we will do little and settle for the mediocre. Our world can't do without those who believe that things ought to be different and should be changed. George Casalis once made the comment, 'I am resolved to persevere in unconditionally refusing to accept the intolerable'.

The marks of passion can be seen around us in sports figures, artists, musicians and social reformers. And those of a deeply religious persuasion who have left their mark on the world were men and women of passion as well: Gandhi, Desmond Tutu, Mother Teresa and Martin Luther King, Jr.

But to live life with passion is no smooth and easy road. In fact, it is fraught with difficulties. Little wonder that many prefer to live life another way. And so often, we hear the words 'don't get involved', or 'you can't change these things anyway', or 'we need further research'.

One of the difficulties in living with passion is that we need to make sure that we are passionate about the right things. If it is true that love is blind, then passion is blind and deaf. It is possible to be passionate about wrong, or at best one-sided, causes and issues. And it is very easy to become so 'one-eyed' about one's cause that one fails to see the bigger picture or the problems of one's own cause.

In the light of this, we always need to remind ourselves that the two big causes of the Twentieth century and all the passion and commitment that these released in the Western world were patent failures. I refer here to the short-lived Hitler regime and the longer-lived Communism of the Soviet Union. Here passion became perverted. And when passion is cut loose from wholesome ethical norms, it deteriorates into a diabolical idolatry.

Passion, therefore, must be infused by a moral vision. It can't simply be reactive. Passion can only be a passion for the good—never for evil.

I believe that the biblical story is the expression of God's good for humans and for our world. To live that vision with passion will challenge us to live a life of reconciliation, forgiveness, service to humanity, empowerment of the poor, work for justice and resistance of the powers of oppression.

But to live this vision with passion is a costly and difficult journey. There are always the forces of opposition, the possibility of discouragement and the temptation to be co-opted. Martin Luther King, Jr.'s mission for racial reconciliation is both fulfilled—legislation is in place—and unfinished—there are still deep racial divides and ethnic marginalizations.

One of the things that has struck me again is how naïve we often are and how easily we give up. While we recognize that it takes generations to build good social values and institutions and that it takes an equally long time for good things to become corrupted and eventually perverted, we assume that change for the better can occur quickly. Passion cannot be a short burst of enthusiasm while one is young and has few commitments and responsibilities. Passion needs to be the formative influence for the whole journey. The work for good and for justice is never a hundred-meter sprint. It is a marathon. Therefore, our passions can't be rooted in passion itself. They need to be rooted in a credible vision and in hope and faith.

commitment: its challenges and pains

As I have mentioned before, Naasicaa, your great grandfather settled in Brisbane, Australia on leaving The Netherlands. He has never moved from Brisbane and lived all his life in the family home. His has been a life of settledness. My life has been quite different. I have lived twice in the State of Victoria and twice in Western Australia, besides spending many years in Queensland. I have also lived in the Philippines and Canada and regularly travel to other Asian countries where I teach. My lifestyle has been much more nomadic.

My lifestyle rather than my father's is becoming more the norm in our contemporary world. With a global economy, the world is literally on the move, not only with the vast movement of raw materials, agriculture and consumer products, but also with people. Our societies in the Western world, as a result, have become multi-cultural. It is highly probable that after finishing your undergraduate studies in Australia you will do graduate work elsewhere. You will also follow every young Australian's dream to travel and see the world. And in your lifetime you may well live on several continents and in turn pursue up to four or five different careers. The usual scenario added to this mobility is that many people also track through a number of serious relationships and several marriages. I hope the latter won't be true of you.

The vast mobility that characterizes our world is not only full of excitement and interest; it also has all sorts of unfortunate consequences. So much travel has ecological consequences. And the more one moves, the more one becomes disconnected from people and place. We become modern nomads with little sense of connectedness to neighbourhood, church, institutions and political structures.

Mobility, the increasing diversity of our urban environments, our lack of regard for major social institutions and the self-interest that so characterizes our mind-set and values have made the notion of solidarity and its companion, commitment, very difficult ideas. And yet commitment is a part of the fabric of human community and of relationships. It's something we need to talk about.

Let me start, Naasicaa, as I often do, with a theological starting point. Theology for me is not an area of interest that is for the clergy alone. Thinking theologically—or as Harry Blamires puts it, thinking Christianly—involves thinking about all of life from the perspective of the biblical story.[5] This is important for me, for it is the story of God and of God's Wisdom.

What is striking about that story is this commitment or covenant that lies at its very heart. God makes covenant with us and 'his' commitment to us is one of grace, generosity and fidelity. The Old Testament book of Deuteronomy puts it so clearly: 'But it was because the Lord loved you and kept the oath he swore to your forefathers that he brought you out with a mighty hand and redeemed you from the land of slavery . . . know therefore that the Lord your God is God; he is the faithful God keeping his covenant of love to a thousand generations . . .' (7:8–9).

Commitment in the biblical story is not premised on the mutual maintenance of the commitment, or, in other words, on the idea: I will *only* be faithful if you are. Rather, it is based on the veracity of God's faithfulness, which converts our unfaithfulness into a fragile faithfulness and walk of obedience.

I think this central motif has implications for the way we are to operate in the world. We don't operate with a debit/credit morality. Our stance is not: 'I will love you to the degree that you love me', but rather 'I will love in good and bad times'. This is not in any way to deny that healthy relationships have to do with mutual self-giving and receiving. But relationships do go through difficulties and cycles. There are times where the one will need to give more than the other.

In the earlier part of this letter, I proposed that we live in a largely passionless world. I think we also live in a world where commitment is a difficult reality for us. It is difficult not only because of the factors I have mentioned above, but also because we have the idea that a commitment must primarily benefit me. So the thinking goes: 'I will be committed to the company, as long as it will further my career'. Or, 'I will be committed to this relationship, as long as it satisfies my needs'.

While I am not wanting to deny that there should also be something in it for us, we cannot make commitments solely on the basis of how they will benefit us. What about the company I work for? And what about the other person in the relationship?

In thinking this through, I believe we need to move away from the old idea of hierarchies of commitment. In a much older world, people followed the hierarchy of King, landlord and family, in that order. In the modern era, it has been family, job and country. And in more recent times, it has been myself, with all other hierarchies falling into other places depending on their potential benefit to me. In contemporary Christian thinking the hierarchy of commitment has been God, family, church and world. The thinking here is that I first should be loyal and committed to God, then to my family and so on. This may sound good, but it is fundamentally faulty. Moreover, it is unlivable. One can't 'divvy' up life like that.

This kind of thinking is faulty because it goes against the tenor of the biblical story, where we are invited to love God and neighbour, and even our enemies. Moreover, we are invited to outwork our commitment to God by serving our family, our colleagues at work and the wider community. Furthermore, there may be times when we have to give one area of responsibility greater attention. In a certain phase in our life, that may be family. In another phase, that may be the wider community.

The problem with hierarchies of commitment is that whatever is down at the bottom receives the least attention. That gets the leftovers of our time, energy and attention. So if we live the God, family, church and world hierarchy, then our involvement with our wider community gets the least attention. A strange idea, when the God of the Bible is a God whose love, passion and commitment is for the world! Sadly, many Christians do attempt to live this hierarchy, usually with the unfortunate consequence that much of the attention is placed on family, and little on the world and little on God. Little wonder that Christians are often socially irrelevant. And it is not surprising that prayer is hardly a part of our lives.

Rather than hierarchies, I think we should live a series of interlocking circles of responsibility, where the one circle impacts the other. My commitment to church should impact my commitment to God, family and world. My commitment to family should impact the other circles and so on. This reflects much more the interconnectedness of life and the holistic nature of our mission in the world. Moreover, this means that family can also be a resource of service to the world and not simply the place of withdrawal from the world. Furthermore, our involvement with the world can deepen our relationship with God and our relationship with God can deepen our concern for the world. Finally, the church should strengthen the family and not only that, families should enrich the life of the community of faith.

Here, once again, I am suggesting that we need to live much more dialectically and not hierarchically. In drawing near to God in prayer, solitude and contemplation, I should not leave the world behind. I should take it with me—my family, neighbours and the pain of the world. Moreover, in meeting God in the quiet place of reflection, I meet with a God whose passion and commitment is for the world. This God turns my face raised in contemplation and adoration to the challenges and needs of the world and invites me to serve bread and wine to others and wash the feet of the world.[6] Conversely, in my connectedness to neighbour, workplace and wider community, and in responding to the beauty and needs of our world, I am drawn to God for 'his' wisdom, grace and empowerment.

One of the comments that I regularly hear is that we don't have time to live this way. Family and work already fill our lives and with the increasing pressures and demands of the workplace, there is no time left for wider involvement. I accept that these pressures are real. I experience them myself. But I don't agree with the conclusions we draw, namely, that we don't have time for other things. We can make time, if we are willing to sacrifice in other areas. And that I think gets to the heart of the issue. We want a lot in terms of a good lifestyle and are, as a consequence, not willing to live more carefully so we can make commitments to issues that are beyond the parameters of our own self-interest. If we only make commitments to ourselves and not to wider issues and the common good, then we are in fact contributing to the social fragmentation of our society.

To live our commitments is no easy road. In other people's commitment to us, we receive. In our commitments to others, we give. Such is the reciprocity of life. But as I have said earlier, commitments can't work on a ledger morality, where you give first and then I give an equal amount back! There are times when we may have to give more, or times when we need to receive more. There are also times when our sense of commitment weakens, for in the real world things are refractory. Our work environment or our interpersonal relationships may become especially difficult and so our resolve can weaken.

We have to be willing to 'hang in' during both the good and difficult times. This is especially true when we are involved in the bigger social justice causes of our day. Nothing gets easily fixed up. We have to be willing to be there for the long haul.

facing disillusionment

It is very likely that we will become discouraged in working out our commitments. This may come our way for many reasons. We may have over-committed ourselves. This calls for re-evaluation and becoming more realistic regarding what we can do. We may have run out of steam at a particular point and instead of carrying others we may need to be carried for a while. But it is also possible that we have become disillusioned.

This touches a core issue in the outworking of our commitments. We often hope for much—too much! We expect our friends to be consistently loyal, our lover to be wonderfully sexy, our boss to be fair and our social institutions to serve us well. There is little doubt that we will be disappointed. And disappointment may lead to disillusionment. For some, this leads to anger against others and possible retaliation.

We have to face this as part of the human experience. And while this may temporarily stop us in our tracks, we must not allow it to derail us. Disillusionment hardens the arteries of love and hope and breeds the sterile seeds of cynicism.

As a result, we need to develop a spirituality that faces failure. While we may want things to turn out well, this does not always occur. And so, we have to learn to remain committed even when things don't always work out as we had hoped. Of course, I am not talking about remaining committed to relationships or causes that are inherently destructive. But I am talking about remaining committed in the face of difficulty, resistance and lack of success.

Success may be the fruit of our commitment, but can never be the basis for our commitment. Instead, commitments are made because we believe that we are called to give ourselves to certain persons, causes and situations. But not all commitments are ones of choice. Our lover or our work may be, but to be committed to parents or children is a commitment that is placed into our hands.

Like everything else, commitments have a renewable quality. They need to be made again and again to the same person or cause. And to do that, we need to find renewed love and hope.

a personal reflection

I am the kind of person who takes a lot of time to make a commitment in friendship or to a cause. I am slow. And I dare not rush into things that I cannot sustain. I realize that other people may operate very differently. And that is okay. But once I have made a commitment, I am willing to hang in, even when the going gets really tough. And because I am more of a realist than an idealist, I don't bring too great a set of expectations with me. I see myself as vulnerable, others as fragile in spite of their abilities and strengths, and the world as refractory and difficult.

Relationships aside, I believe that our best commitments should bear the limits of time. Commitment to causes, projects, work and ministry assignments are best executed with a sense of seeking to make a contribution for a significant period of time and then moving on. I don't mean moving on when the going gets tough. What I mean is making commitments that facilitate and empower others, so that one has to face the happy and difficult task of handing things over and leaving it to others to carry the project forward. This is a powerful lesson in relinquishment. Unfortunately, some good people are so committed to causes that they don't know when to get out of the way!

I loved the six years teaching at the Asian Theological Seminary in Manila. I could easily have stayed there forever. But my last two years were committed to team teaching so that others could take over certain areas of responsibility. I cried a lot during that time; it is not easy to let go. But life is as much about relinquishments as it is about accomplishments.

gratitude, wonder, creativity and the dulling power of conformity

letter eleven

I did not grow up with a lot of emphasis on creativity, even though my mother enjoyed singing and my father was a choir master. Life had its regular routines and its yearly holidays at the beach, where I felt as free as the seagulls present with ever watchful eye for the gutting of fish caught in the Noosa River, north of Brisbane.

At a young age, I swapped my violin for soccer boots and sport became the passion of my life. I am glad I became passionate about that, because beside my deep love for nature, I was bored with much of family life, schooling and church. At school, when I quickly finished my classroom assignments, I was allowed to work in the school yard to prepare the antbed tennis court for the ladies social tennis events. In church, there was no escape.

How different things have been for you, Naasicaa. Art classes, music, drama and dancing have been the tone and texture of your life and that of your sister, Annasophia. But then little wonder, with your mother being a fine arts graduate!

I begin this letter on this note, but I in no way wish to suggest that creativity can only be expressed in these ways. Nor do I believe that creativity has only to do with music, art and drama. Rather, creativity encapsulates the whole human enterprise from design to manufacture; from dreams to the beauty of buildings, institutions and cities; from passion to the work of social justice; from commitment to the work of agriculture; from care to the work of healing and medical intervention. There is no aspect of life which is not etched with the colours of creativity, whether that be the art of loving, the joy of home-making, the shaping of our environment or the building of communities and institutions.

the roots of creativity

However, I think you would agree, Naasicaa, that creativity is not where one begins. Creativity is more the fruit of one's life and not the root, even though one may innately have creative gifts. It is possible for one's creativity not to come to full expression. It may even remain submerged. It is also possible for one's creativity to be put to useless, unconstructive or even downright criminal pursuits. Some criminals are just so clever and have converted their abilities to serve the ignoble and the offensive.

So if we don't start with creativity, where do we begin? We could begin with the wonder of who we are and with gratitude for the gift of life and of all that is good in our world. Other starting points, of course, are also

possible. But I believe that these two terms—gratitude and
wonder—are key to our discussion. No real creativity is
possible if it does not come from love and thankfulness.
While a person full of anger or cynicism can bring forth
'things', this will hardly be a form of creativity that makes
life whole. Moreover, if one's heart and mind are not open
with wonder, then creativity may well remain dormant.

In one of my other letters, I hinted at the fact that
I believe that gratitude is one of the most fundamental
postures of life, and that this posture is life-giving.
Gratitude recognizes the fundamental giftedness of life
and the nature of the human community. It also recognizes
the rich texture of relationships as the web through which
we receive so much. And overarching all of this is the
acknowledgement and celebration of the God from whom
all good gifts come.

To be a grateful person implies not only that one
is thankful, but more particularly that one is open and
receptive. To live with a sense of gratitude means that one
appreciates what one has. One can celebrate the moment,
enjoy the event, appreciate the gift, rejoice in the kindness
of the giver. As a result, one is not always focusing on what
one does *not* have. Gratitude nullifies the jealous glance at
others and what they have.

Gratitude serves creativity. It is the mother of the
good, for it helps us see and make use of what we have
been given. But gratitude also makes us open towards the
future. Having been given much, we are not only called to
bless others, but are also encouraged to remain open to
being further enriched. Good things come not to those who
demand, assert and manipulate, but to those who are able
to receive and give.

To live with gratitude is to live out of grace and the
sustaining and empowering presence of the Holy Spirit, who

enhances our natural talents with charisms—those special gifts of creativity, reconciliation, healing and insight.

Since our contemporary culture makes so much of consumer products as the means to a sense of well-being and, in many cases, a sense of identity, we should ask whether gratitude and much-having are closely related. It is good to explore this issue. But I did not, first of all, have this in mind. My focus is more on gratitude for *who* we are rather than on *what* we possess. By who we are I mean our physicality, personality, talents, intelligence, beliefs, values, the goodness and love that is in our lives and the way we operate in the world. I have in view our passions and the things that move us. This is more fundamental. And what we have, in terms of material possessions and money, is for me a very secondary matter.

If you were to ask, Naasicaa, your mother will tell you that for most of her growing up years, our family lived on a financial shoestring. This was not because we did not have the training and skills to work in well-paid jobs. But we had chosen to live differently. By 'we' I primarily mean your grandmother and I. As an aside, I do need to tell you that we often struggled with implicating our children, including your mother, in our life choices. It is one thing for parents to make certain choices, but these do implicate the children in their formative years. And when the parents make some hard choices, should these be foisted onto the children? So we are still wondering whether we served our children well. I think there are areas where we failed.

But let me come back to the main line of my discussion and talk about what this different lifestyle looked like. We lived a life of downward mobility, hospitality and Christian community serving homeless young people and those with drug-related problems. We lived in rented houses, practised a simple lifestyle and had enough to meet our basic needs. We grew vegetables, baked our own bread and operated a food co-operative for the various community houses. There was little cash, but lots of life.

And there was gratitude and creativity. We played games, had poetry reading evenings, did pottery, had lots of picnics, film evenings, discussion nights, bush walking. Once a week, we had a special meal—a sort of Christian love feast, with lots of good food, readings, candles and lots of fun and storytelling.[1]

One night a week there were art classes in one of the community homes. It was amazing to see young people, who basically felt hopeless about themselves, discover that they had artistic abilities. They also came to appreciate the beauty of nature. They learned to care for animals on one of our farms. Others grew through the challenges of mountain climbing.

So, Naasicaa, gratitude and much-having in terms of material possessions are not necessarily connected. But having a richness of life in terms of relationships, sharing and creativity are very much related. We experienced the latter and largely lacked the former.

One of the things that struck me during my years in the Philippines was that the slums of the poor were places of hope rather than the ghettos of despair. There was laughter, love and gratitude. And that was because there was a sense of solidarity and sharing. Suffering and difficulty throw people together. Material possessions were skimpy. But much-having is not the basis for happiness nor for the joy of gratitude.

So in the West, we have things the wrong way round. When we loudly proclaim to ourselves and to the rest of the world that one needs much in order to be happy and grateful, we are communicating a distorted message. Our much-having has only produced a culture of complaint. We always want more and are never satisfied. We are willing to sacrifice health and our relationships in the quest to have more. We end up living diminished lives and gratitude does not texture the fabric of our being.

wonder

In the above part of my letter, I have been talking about gratitude as a fundamental posture of life. I believe that thankfulness is life-giving. Gratitude acknowledges both the goodness of God and the way others have enriched us. I am also suggesting that gratitude has everything to do with creativity. Thankfulness, marked by joy and love, always seeks to express itself in ways that enrich others. And for me, that is the heart of creativity. It matters little whether that comes to expression in the way we prepare a meal, decorate our homes, make love, write poetry, do a painting, reform a political party or write a new theology. The possibilities are endless.

I also touched on the notion of wonder as intrinsic to creativity. But before exploring that theme, there are two important qualifiers I need to make. The one is that I am not implying that creativity does not involve hard work and the development of skills. Of course, it does. Creativity does not mean that one does not need to become proficient in a particular skill. Secondly, creativity has other tributaries in addition to the streams of gratitude and wonder. One such stream is pain. From difficulty and disappointment, redeemed from their propensity towards despair and bitterness, good things can come. But more of that in another letter.

To wonder has a kaleidoscope of meanings. It means to be open to the new, unexpected and extraordinary, to be astonished at something, to question, doubt and speculate. There is an amazing sense of openness in all of this. And it is so different than the tasks we are usually so busy with: to study, to do, to work, to achieve, to prepare, to complete. Do we make time to wonder? Do you know how to wonder?

I have mentioned in a previous letter Max Weber's point about the rational efficiency of the West. We all experience its impact. Our education system sees its task as preparing us to become skillful and efficient, and the workplace soon maximizes this.

This rational efficiency characterizes every dimension of urban life—our transport systems, housing, work environments and health care. Even our time at the gym is marked by this efficiency. And, of course, we work on the logic that efficiency will enhance productivity, that productivity will bring about prosperity and that prosperity will bring about happiness. I think, Naasicaa, that you will have gained the impression by now that I question the movement of this logic.

But just as we have to move away from being a culture of complaint, we also have to move away from our much-doing and become more contemplative. I have touched on this in my letter on spirituality, but let me return to it here, for it is what wonder is all about. And wonder is the seedbed of creativity, just as contemplation is the mistress of radicality and the source of transformation.

To wonder requires a free outer space. And in the frenetic cycle of home responsibilities, work, further training, church, entertainment and the pursuit of particular interests, free space has become the luxury we can no longer afford. In fact, our culture tells us to fill every moment in order to gain every experience. I believe the opposite is desperately necessary. We need to create empty places in the corridors and passageways of our lives. Therefore, we need to recover the practice of solitude.

Jacques Ellul once made the observation that the first duty of free people is to say, 'No'. Our culture tells us the opposite: the first duty of happy people is to say, 'Yes'.[2] And yet, if we are ever to rediscover the gentle art of wondering, we must learn to say 'no' so we can preserve empty spaces in our lives.

To wonder also requires a free inner space. This is more fundamental and usually precedes the creation of a free outer space. The two are related: the quiet outer place can help create an inner detachment and openness.

A free inner space has many contours. One is a willingness to be alone. Aloneness is not the same as loneliness. While loneliness is often the experience of sadness because of lack of company, aloneness can be a positive experience. We choose to be by ourselves in order to be quiet, to reflect, to listen to our heart, to pray. Secondly, a free inner space is the place of the listening heart. There is much that we brush aside. There are dreams we fail to listen to. Intuitions that we rationalize. Feelings that we repress. Hopes that we squash. Moreover, we often fail to hear the whispers of the Spirit. Thirdly, this inner space needs to be beyond ideology, where we are willing to look at the cracks in the systems of meaning we have created for ourselves and be open to rethinking what we hold so dearly and securely.

There is great power in wondering: Do I need to think, be and live this way? Is this really the meaning and purpose of life? Are these really the ways in which we should act in our world? Are these the sorts of values we should hold? Are these the kinds of institutions we should build and maintain? The questions, of course, are endless. But to wonder is to ask new questions, including the hard and disturbing ones.[3] To wonder, above all, is to be open to surprise. Things do happen without our planning. Good things do come our way. In fact, in the story of God, we see most clearly that God is a God of surprises. The unexpected occurs: grace instead of judgment, the blessedness of the poor, the power of the weak.

conformity

I have mentioned in another letter that we pride ourselves on being free agents in our Western world. I believe that this is far from the case. We are under tremendous pressure to accept, imbibe and live the dominant values of our culture. We are regarded as being odd if we don't believe all the hype about progress, all the banalities about success, all the promises regarding consumerism.

Radicality has become a dirty word in the contemporary world. Radicals are simply ratbags. And whether they are the leftover socialists or hippies of a previous era, they have nothing to say to our present context. In our kind of world, both those on the political left and right have moved to an insipid grey intermediate zone.

To live with gratitude is to appreciate and to celebrate the good that is in our lives, families, institutions and world. But gratitude does not condone evil—it does not live with a happiness and joy that is blind to the pain of our world. Similarly, to live with wonder is not to wander off into some cocooned inner psychic state. To live with wonder is not a form of escapism. It is, instead, a deeply contemplative experience, where we question what is, dream of the new and have the courage to move to a creative praxis.

Appeals are constantly made that we bend to the altar of conformity in the name of harmony and peace. But harmony is not uniformity, nor is it bland compliance. Harmony, instead, is the fruit of the convergence of opposites, which produces unity in diversity. Harmony bears the hallmark of creativity, while the peace of conformity is a false truce. There is nothing lasting about relationships which are based on the suppression of real feelings and thoughts.

a personal reflection

As you know, Naasicaa, I have worked for many years in several church related institutions. I have never found these to be particularly open places. Many repeated phrases come to mind: 'This is how we counsel here'; 'This is what we believe'; 'This is our ministry focus'.

I have no problem with organizations having a particular mission and purpose. But I have a problem with the idea that one's mission can only be fulfilled in a particular way. Not only is it appropriate to ask whether things could be done better or differently, but it is even more appropriate to ask whether we are really serving well the people we are called to serve.

This can so easily drop out of view. Social welfare services can sometimes give more attention to their staff than to the clients they seek to assist. Universities often give greater attention to the research agendas of its professors than to the teaching and training of students. And churches can sometimes give so much attention to their members that they neglect the seeker and the stranger.

Thus creativity is called for in order to maintain healthy organizations and find better ways to serve those who come for help, education or fellowship and nurture.

Creativity is the endeavour to renew what is old and create the signposts of the new so that life will be more whole. In other words, creativity has to do with bringing into being all that is good and all that reflects the intention of the Creator.

I am back in Brisbane. The winter sun is making its early demise into the bowels of the earth. But at this very point its rays refracted through dark clouds on the horizon are the most vivid. There is great beauty in the world of nature. And following the invitation of the Creator, we are called to add to the world's beauty by the way we live, by what we make and in the things we create.

While conformity to the good is good, we are so often invited to conform to dominant values that are less than what the good could be. Hence the power of wonder and creativity can dynamite the dulling power of conformity and offer up new ways of being and doing.

Within a Christian frame this has to do with the renewing work of the Holy Spirit, who brings us to Christ, refurbishes our inner being, graces us with gifts and enables us to reconfigure communities of faith which seek to transform our world.

mending and bending

letter twelve

I have been wondering, Naasicaa, what you have thought about my letters. You know that I have not wanted to give you trite advice, nor have I wanted to make things easy or simplistic, because I don't think life is like that.

Oh yes, like you, I do know people who seem to rollick along happily. But that is not true for most of us. I have been counselling people for too long to know that life is not a picnic for most people. There are the deep questions of self-identity: am I really okay and can I accept and be at peace with myself? There are the questions of relationship: do others really love me and can I love them? Furthermore, there are the questions of vocation: what do I really want to be and do? Then there are the questions of values: how will I conduct myself in the world and by what set of ethics will I shape my lifestyle? And finally, there are the questions of ultimacy: what do I really believe about this life and the life to come? And these sets of questions are not even exhaustive!

These and the other matters that I have raised in my other letters probably all sound a bit too 'heavy'. Maybe you are right. I do tend to take life a little too seriously. Maybe this has something to do with my Dutch roots and my Calvinist heritage. Or maybe it is simply my personality. It is true, though, that one's personality has a lot to do with the way one sees, engages and experiences life. One of my good friends, who goes back to the early days of our work in inner city mission, is an 'eternal optimist'. For him life is good, God is good, problems virtually do not exist and everything is possible. But other friends of mine have seen and experienced life in tragic terms: always the dark side, always difficulty, always a drama, always the experience of pain.

I am quite sure that I do not fit into either of these two ends of the spectrum. I like to see myself as a realist impregnated with hope. I take life seriously, but also know how to dance. I do hope that some of that 'lightness of being' has come through in my letters. But not enough, possibly? Maybe the tread of my heavy boots has squashed the flowers. If that is so and if that is the impression you have gained from my letters, then my letters have been a communication failure. I may have only reinforced the general impression that religious people are at best dour and, at worst, dreadfully boring and irrelevant!

I need to tell you, though, that that is *not* how I have experienced the Christian life. It has been quite different. To put it in a nutshell, it has been an experience of a myriad of colours. I experience the joy of God's presence and goodness. I experience the pain of the cross, which calls me to repentance, discipleship and service. I have an abiding sense of thankfulness for all that has been given. And I am constantly stretched and challenged to live the life of faith in our kind of world—the First World with its skepticism and the Third World with the pain of injustice. That doesn't sound too dour, does it? I hope not.

In touching on these matters, I am really on the way to probing some other dimensions of life and of the Christian faith. If I was to put it really crudely, the question would be, 'Is the life of faith fundamentally one of blessing and joy, or one of ongoing struggle'? To put it more carefully, the issue is: can I come to wholeness in a broken world? And this is related to the deeper question of how much the grace of God transforms my life. In theology, this is the question of sanctification.

a theology of mending

In several of my previous letters, Naasicaa, I have spoken of a fundamental goodness in our lives and in our world. But I have also touched on the dark side. It is always easier to see this on the mega-screen of history. Unjust wars, irrational racial hatreds, blatant exploitation. The list is long and singularly painful. How can we do these things to each other? And why do we do them again and again? Thus our contemporary history will remain pock-marked by Hiroshima, the Gulag, Auschwitz and the Rwandan and Balkan madness. Pock-marked is, of course, a deliberate misuse of language. I am really talking about deep craters.

What is less clear is to understand and to come to terms with the dark side *within us*. We all have our aberrations. For some, these are irrational fears. For others, these are compulsive behaviours. And some experience unidentified angers. Here also the list is endless. But these things both hurt us and affect our relationship with others. Thus these very personal and even private matters spill out into our world.

Whether these things are caught through the socialization process, or whether they are part of an archetypal substructure as propounded by Jung, the reality of these things is hardly fully explained.[1] The biblical story makes it clear that sin is part of the human condition. And this has affected us all, in all of our relationships. No part of life is secluded from the effects of wrongdoing.

But as I have pointed out in a previous letter, the story of God is a story of God's healing and renewing activity. In the words of the feminist theologian Letty Russell, God has in view the mending of all creation.[2] This means not only our personal lives, but also our communities and finally the whole of reality in the creation of new heavens and a new earth.

At the personal level, this mending means the reparation of our relationship with God, the renewal of our inner being and growth in maturity and a desire to bless others. The healing of our communities is the move from fear, suspicion, antagonism and conflict to relationships and structures that are marked by forgiveness, equality and empowerment. And the full healing of the nations is God's final restoration in the eschatological future.

There is no suggestion in the biblical story that this healing process comes to full expression in the here and now. There is no hint of perfection. In the words of Francis Schaeffer there is, however, substantial healing for our personal lives and communities. Thus wholeness remains as much a goal as it is a growing reality.

When we speak of a theology of mending we are referring to an articulation of God's restorative activity. And we may primarily set this in the creation-chaos-recreation paradigm.

A good and beautiful world is God's gift to humanity. This gift is to be appreciated and cared for within the framework of a life of love, worship and obedience to the generous Giver, the Lord of life, the God of creation.

This frame becomes shattered due to human folly and disobedience. We thought we knew better. We had our own ideas about using this gift. Thus humanity went its own way and pulled in its wake the ever widening ripples of distortion.

Starting from the personal centre of a rebellious 'I will go my own way', human wrong-doing spilled in all directions. What a waste! What folly! And everything becomes affected and infected. Distortion occurs in every dimension of life, including our interpersonal relationships and our relationship to the created order.

Of course, from our side, our relationship to God particularly becomes twisted. We become creatures in flight from the generous Giver. And in order to justify our folly we hide, deny and rationalize. The ultimate form of this outrageous rationalization is to suggest that we don't need this God or that this God is fundamentally dictatorial and oppressive. Modern humanism in particular seeks to cast God in such terms.

So we bend things. We have made chaos in our world, whether we have done that personally or corporately. We have bent our view of God and our relationship to 'him'. And so we have ended up with the idea that health and well-being is premised on human autonomy. True freedom is to be free from dependency upon God and, by extension, dependency upon others. This has distorted our view of the human person. Instead of being persons in relationship with God and others and living in community and cooperation for the glory of God and the common good, we have pitted ourselves against each other. We have become individuals in competition rather than persons in mutual cooperation.

This pitting ourselves against others has also occurred on a much grander scale in the many wars of acquisition and the various forms of colonialism of the recent past. It hardly needs to be pointed out that this also lies at the heart of global trade and the capitalist enterprise.

The idea that we bend things sounds a bit harsh. Don't we build good cities and institutions? The answer to this is a resounding, 'Yes'! We do a lot of good in our world. And for this we are thankful and may see this as a diffusion of God's common grace in our world.

But the very good that we do also has and brings about its own distortions. We do good for selfish reasons. Our good is often what is good *for us* and not for others. And our good, rather than leading us to celebrate the God of all goodness, often leads us to celebrate our own human autonomy. Thus our very goodness leads us away from rather than towards God.

As a consequence we need to be mended. In healing lies our hope. In God's recreative activity lies our renewal.

Human disobedience brought deep sadness to the heart of God, but not a sullen withdrawal. Nor was humanity left to its own stupidities. The God of the Bible is the ever loving and ever seeking God. God seeks us out in our sinfulness, finds us in our waywardness and welcomes us home from our wanderings.

God's restorative activity is intended to mend us, to make us whole. And everywhere on the pages of the Bible we hear this amazing theme: 'I am the Lord, who heals you' (Exodus 15:26b); God is a 'refuge for the poor . . . a shelter from the storm and a shade from the heat' (Isaiah 25:4a); God 'forgives all your sins and heals all your diseases' (Psalm 103:3); 'I will give you a new heart and put a new spirit in you' (Ezekiel 36:26a). This restorative activity is summed up in the benediction: 'May God himself, the God of peace, sanctify you through and through. May your whole spirit, soul and body be kept blameless at the coming of our Lord Jesus Christ. The one who calls you is faithful and he will do it' (1 Thessalonians 5:23–24).

God's mending activity is costly. It is God reaching beyond the chasm into our need through self-identification. God both enters our need and engages our sinfulness by becoming the bearer of our waywardness and woundedness.

The prophet Isaiah saw this with a revelatory clarity: 'Surely he took up our infirmities and carried our sorrows . . . he was pierced for our transgressions, he was crushed for our iniquities; the punishment that brought us peace was upon him and by his wounds we are healed' (Isaiah 53:4–5). John the gospel writer reiterates this theme. Jesus speaks of himself in the following terms: 'I am the good shepherd . . . and I lay down my life for the sheep' (John 10:14–15). And Paul sings, as it were, that we are 'justified freely by his grace through redemption that came by Christ Jesus' (Romans 3:24).

Since the fall into chaos the whole of God's activity has been restorative. God has bent 'himself' towards us. And in Christ Jesus, 'he' has most fully and clearly displayed 'his' love and desire to make us whole and to call us back to 'his' original intention.

dimensions of healing

I am back in Yangon. It's the rainy season and it's bucketing down. I am worried that some of my friends' homes will be flooded. The place where they live has poor drainage, and they are also struggling to survive economically. By comparison I am well off. This draws attention to the fact that life is in many ways unfair, the world is characterized by injustice, and healing in the broader sense of that term still needs to occur.

When we speak of the themes of healing or mending drawn from the biblical story, we are amazed by its comprehensiveness. Healing is not simply the absence of sickness, but the well-being of life lived in the presence of God. The theme of well-being must not be interpreted to mean that we will have all we want and will experience smooth sailing on life's journey.

The primary healing that is accented in the pages of the Bible is spiritual healing. Here I am speaking about the restoration and deepening of our relationship with God as Father, Son and Holy Spirit. There are many ways of expressing this. We can speak of 'coming to faith'. We can also call this one's 'conversion'. I prefer the language of 'homecoming'. Paul the apostle uses this kind of imagery. He speaks of us being 'separate from Christ, excluded from citizenship in Israel and foreigners to the covenants of promise . . . but now in Christ Jesus you who once were far away have been brought near through the blood of Christ' (Ephesians 2:12-13).

What is amazing is that not only do we come home to God in repentance and faith, but God also comes home to us. John, the gospel writer, puts this most beautifully: 'Jesus replied, "If anyone loves me, he will obey my teaching. My Father will love him and we will come to him and make our home with him"' (John 14:24).

In the light of this we can say that spiritual healing or coming to faith is entering into a living relationship with God as a community of persons: Father, Son and Holy Spirit.

The deepening of this relationship is what the ongoing journey of faith is all about. The great classics of Christian spirituality testify to the way in which women and men have sought to understand the process of growing in Christian maturity and deepening one's union with God.[3]

A further theme in the process of mending is relational healing. I have the horizontal dimensions of life in view, but I believe that this is related to the vertical, the restoration of our relationship with God.

Relational healing has to do with all those exciting and difficult processes of building communities of faith, family, friendships and various institutions. It also has to do with neighbourliness and the practice of good citizenship. Relational healing involves a willingness to open our lives to others in loving service and care, but also to receive help, encouragement, support and advice from others.

This form of mending recognizes the interrelatedness of life. And in the ethos of Ubuntu Theology developed by Desmond Tutu, among others, it celebrates the key idea that the well-being of the one involves the well-being of many.[4] I am not truly blessed if others are not blessed, and I am not truly free unless there is freedom for others.

In the biblical story it is clear that God builds a people.[5] The restoration of human relationships out of the quagmire of fear, insecurity, distrust and disregard is a great blessing that shapes the fabric of community. Thus relational healing is essential to community building.

It is a significant theme in the biblical story that friendship with God means friendship with others. Love of God is to issue into love of neighbour and even the love of one's enemy.

Our link with Christ through the Spirit also joins us to the body of Christ, the community of faith, where a diversity of people are made one in Christ (1 Corinthians 12:12–13; Galatians 3:26–28). And we are encouraged to live out the mystery that the way we love and care for others is an expression of our love for God. The words from Matthew's gospel are pertinent: 'Whatever you do for one of the least of these brothers of mine, you did for me' (Matthew 25:40).

I hope, Naasicaa, as you have been reading this you will have noticed how different these accents are to the values of contemporary culture. Our Western culture has elevated the importance of the rights and needs of the individual. There is little vision for community building and working for the common good. Individual achievement rather than relationality is the big focus.

It is my hope that you will be a mender and community builder. Building relationships of cooperation that draw people together for the common good is what I hope your life will be about.

This has become a long letter, so let me briefly touch on some other dimensions of healing before I come back to the topic of injustice.

Reading the gospels with its focus on the person and mission of Jesus, it is clear that healing and exorcism were blessings that Jesus sought to impart. While I am fully appreciative of the role of medicine and counselling in healing, I believe that there is a continuing need for prayer. In prayer we may seek the renewing presence of the Holy Spirit for people's inner woundedness and for those areas of their lives where the powers of darkness have gained some form of access.

To the degree that one can make a snapshot of the global church, there appear to be signs of recovery in praying for people in these ways. Here also the work of mending is taking place.

What is more difficult to understand is in what ways the healing of a neighbourhood, or even national healing, may occur, particularly given the pluralism of contemporary society. And to broaden the picture, it is appropriate to ask in what ways healing can come to nations experiencing poverty, exploitation and injustice. It seems that all the work of community development and aid is not significantly changing the global face of poverty.[6]

I do make this a matter of prayer particularly because some of my Asian friends live in such circumstances. And I also attempt to do my bit in poverty alleviation, but I most frequently feel discouraged. Thus healing within society and healing among the nations remains ever so problematical for me.

But I must leave things here. I am excited about God's renewing presence. I believe that healing does occur in myriad ways, yet I recognize that we also continue to distort things and act in destructive ways. The vision of the Bible for a final healing of all the nations remains a far-off dream as well as a present hope.

work and play in a world of inequality

letter thirteen

I am sure you will have noticed, Naasicaa, how the work we do is often used as a descriptor of our personhood. The first question one gets asked in the company of strangers is, 'What work do you do?'

In other cultures this is very different. The first question is not regarding your job, but who you belong to. Your family or your tribal group is a key indicator regarding who you are.

What the above question in a Western cultural setting indicates is that work is important and work is regarded as a status symbol. Both of these dimensions come as no surprise. The West holds high the value of productivity. Our work, therefore, is a participation in producing, building and maintaining all that sustains a society and produces economic well-being and wealth.

That work is also a status symbol flows from the fact that society rewards unevenly the work that humans do. There is a world of difference between what a CEO of a major corporation earns in contrast to a casual waiter or the garbage collector. And because the economic rewards are different, the impression is given that the person with the 'good' job is somehow a better human being. Or, if that is stretching things just a little too far, at least the person with the good job is regarded as a more capable and effective human being. Work matters.

You have already given some thought to this. The subjects you have chosen at school and now at university reflect your concern to head in a particular career trajectory. And you are hopeful that your initial choice will reflect something of your creativity, interests and abilities. You are also hopeful that this is a good choice in the current job market.

Many other things in this regard are going on for you as well. You hope to make a success of your work and you hope that your work will contribute to the well-being of society, although for some the latter dimension is of little concern.

You will have noticed, Naasicaa, how often I have used the word 'hope'. This is appropriate, for the current work environment is hardly characterized by certainties.

The major societal paradigm shifts from agrarian to industrial and to our current post-industrial realities, together with the development of the global market, have resulted in ever changing demands and opportunities in the workforce. So in writing to you about this matter I am touching on something that is both intrinsic to who we are as human beings and something that is fragile and challenging, given our current economic realities. Work constitutes a large slice of our waking hours and therefore it is a topic that clamours for consideration.

a personal reflection

My Reformed heritage gave me the Protestant work ethic. This view maintained that socially good work was to be done to care for one's family, benefit the company, and prosper society, and all was to be done for the glory of God.[1] One was to work hard, live carefully, save and invest and also use a small proportion of these blessings for the benefit of others. This was largely to be done through the diaconate of the church. This view advocated job stability, economic prudence and social conservatism. My family of origin and extended family lived this vision of life.

While I believe that there is much good in this vision, I did not live its central tenets. This was due to a growing understanding that the Christian faith yields a more radical understanding of the world of work than the one advocated by the Protestant work ethic.

My letter to you will attempt to make clear what I mean by this alternative vision. But at the heart of the matter there lies the idea that living for God in the light of the biblical story places us in an ambivalent relationship to the world of work and its central motivations.

To get ahead of myself, but to make a basic point, what does Jesus' call to Peter to leave his fishing nets and to follow Jesus have in common with job stability, economic prudence and social conservatism? Very little, I would suggest. But, of course, there is much to this story. One can't build a whole set of values on one biblical example.

a theology of work

The starting point for a theology of work lies with God 'himself'. The God of the Bible is not some indolent, disinterested and remote Being, locked into some form of ultimate introspection. Instead, Yahweh, Israel's Creator

God, calls the world into being out of the fullness of 'his' love and deeply concerns 'himself' with all that 'he' has made.

It is important to note that the biblical picture is not only that God creates, but also that God sustains, maintains, nurtures and cares for all that has been called into being.

The larger preoccupation of the biblical story is focussed on God's re-creative activity. With things having gone wrong in God's universe, the work of reparation becomes an important dimension. And so we speak of the *work* of salvation—God's redeeming, healing and renewing activity.

Humans made in God's image have been given the joy and the task of imaging God. That means that in conforming to God and becoming godly, we are to reflect the being, joy, will and purposes of God. And at the heart of these purposes is the sustenance and the re-creation of all that God has made.

I think that you can see, Naasicaa, that this has implications for the way we work in the world. Work, in the light of this vision, has both maintenance and transformational dimensions. We work to sustain life. We engage in meaningful activity to earn our living and care for those within our sphere of responsibility. And this meaningful activity has general benefit for our society. The little part that we play contributes to the greater good of the company we work for and this in turn contributes to the general good in society. Thus work has to do with building and maintaining the human community. This is living the vision of the Genesis mandate (Genesis 1:27–28).

Sadly, something of this perspective tends to be missing among Westerners. We think of work as benefiting me—my career, my security and my family. We seem to have little sense of how we are contributing to a larger whole. And even if we did have this perspective, it would not give us much satisfaction and joy.

So the work of maintenance and sustenance is one dimension of a theology of work. There is, however, more to the story. There is also the work of re-creation, healing and restoration.

There are several important dimensions to this. The one sees living this biblical vision primarily in spiritual terms. What this means is that our work is not only that of banker, lawyer, farmer, office worker and motor mechanic; our work is also that of witness.

This work of witness in all the places we find ourselves, including the workplace, is to draw people's attention to the good news which our forebears have all but forgotten. This is the good news about God's redeeming love in Christ, which makes God present to our lives, spreads the fragrance of grace and goodness into the very fabric of our being, brings us into the freedom of forgiveness and brings healing to the inner woundedness of our lives. Clearly this is not the whole story of spiritual healing and renewal. But it is the core, and I have written to you about this before.

But there is more to the story of re-creation, healing and restoration. It has implications for all of our horizontal relationships. Businesses, organizations and institutions also need renewal. This renewal should not be understood merely in economic terms. Renewal in relationships, more just practices, greater fairness and equity may be some of the dimensions of an organizational healing process.

This work of healing also needs to take place in our fractured families and in our neighbourhoods, where community is so frequently absent. This restorative work can be one's paid employment as social worker, community advocate, clergy person, or organizational consultant. But it can also be something one does within one's job as banker, educator or carpenter.

But there is a third dimension to a theology of work—there is also the work of resistance. Sadly, it is not true that healing and renewal are always welcomed and embraced. So often the work of transformation is resisted. People don't want change. They want the *status quo* to continue. This can occur at all levels in a society. As a consequence, the work of resistance comes into play—a resistance to traditions that stultify impulses for change and renewal. This is visionary and prophetic work.

This work may need to occur in the church when spiritual or ecclesiastical renewal is called for. But the work of resistance is also needed in the political and economic dimensions of life. While maintenance says 'more of the same' and renewal is a loud 'yes' to change, resistance is the emphatic 'no'. No, we will not support this idea, this measure, this strategy! No, we will not cooperate with this policy! No, we will not give our political allegiance to this ideology!

The work of resistance is probably the most difficult work: It is walking the road of the cross.[2]

career and vocation

I think you will have noticed, Naasicaa, that the above theology of work modifies the more traditional understanding of the Protestant work ethic, which tends to focus on the maintenance dimensions of the role and task of work. I am suggesting that the vision of work needs to be re-sculpted to include the transformational and prophetic dimensions of work. In the light of this, I wish to talk with you about the matter of career.

As you know, we speak a lot about carefully choosing one's career path. This means that a person knows what he or she wants to become and then consistently works in that direction. It all has to do with careful strategizing—the right schooling, good pre-employment experience, the right contacts, entering a good employment situation, further training and as a consequence, becoming an expert in one's field of endeavour. This is a good and reasonable scenario, but let me raise some counterpoints to this evolutionary trajectory.

First of all, as a young person, you may not always know what you would like to do career wise. And so you may find that in the midst of moving along a certain trajectory you discover a different work priority and field of endeavour. A lawyer becomes a writer. A business person becomes a clergy person. A medical doctor becomes an artist. In our current fast changing work environment one may end up having four or five different careers in a lifetime.

Secondly, not everything comes to us by way of careful planning and strategizing. We also 'fall' into things. A 'chance' meeting might open up a door of opportunity we had never anticipated.

Thirdly, major life changes will have an effect on what we wish to do with our lives. An accident. An illness. A broken relationship. An inheritance. A new relationship. A spiritual conversion. Any of these or other changes may significantly reorient us in such a way that we begin to explore different employment options.

Finally, as we go through the life cycle from youth to aging, a different sense of what is important and worthwhile may begin to enchant us so that we go into a different vocational direction.

When one operates within a Christian frame of reference, I think it is inappropriate to speak of one's career. It is better to speak of one's vocation, for the orientation then is not so much what I want to do with my life. The focus is different. It is, 'What is God calling me to be and do'? It is, 'How is the Spirit leading me regarding work and service'?

The focus then becomes finding an answer to the question, 'How can I in my work honour God, bless others and serve the wider community'? And this question remains the same for the Christian movie star, politician, business person and clergy person. Answers to this most basic of directional questions won't fall out of the sky. They may well come to us through careful thought, fervent praying, wise advice and the gentle nudges of our intuition.

To do one's work—no matter how great or small, paid or voluntary—out of a sense of calling that seeks to bless the wider community and endeavours to honour God is meaningful work indeed!

the politics of play

Work is indeed important. It is intrinsic to who we are. It is an outworking of having been made in God's image. It is linked to the task of imaging God and making our contribution to the shape and welfare of the community.

But we are not only workers. We are also dreamers. We are also relational creatures. And we know something of the joy of play and the grace of relaxation.

While our society places a lot of emphasis on work, it has also created a huge leisure industry. And healthy work practices know something of the importance of recreation and 'down time'. Thus our secular world, in its own way, practices some aspects of the religious notion of Sabbath, although it has not really understood it.

Let me attempt briefly to explain why I think this is so. The secular world knows the importance of rest, which is one dimension of Sabbath, but it has missed the rest of the meaning. In our society rest operates primarily as a means unto an end—that we will be renewed and empowered for further work. The religious notion of Sabbath, by way of contrast, sees Sabbath as an end itself. Sabbath is not simply 'down time'. It is instead entering 'new time'. It is a reorientation from the demands and challenges of daily existence to contemplation and worship.[3]

Sabbath is a refocusing on God as Creator and Sustainer of all things. It is celebrating God's redemptive activity within the community of faith. And it is a symbol to remind us that grace precedes law, that receptivity precedes giving and that contemplation precedes service.

Within a religious frame one begins the week with Sabbath and from that fundamental starting point moves into work. This means that worship, contemplation, playfulness, listening, and receptivity are foundational to being human, and that work is the outflow of this. In the secular sphere, by contrast, one begins with work and ends in much needed rest.

Thus life is not just about work. It is also about gazing, dreaming, playing, hoping, praying. I believe that the politics of play are essential to human creativity. Contemplation and playfulness allow us to disconnect from the tyranny of ever demanding work. These disciplines of the inner being allow us to see things differently and help us to overcome the pressures of our compulsive and frenetic world.

the reign of god and the human enterprise

letter fourteen

I am back in Manila for a few weeks teaching several courses at Asian Theological Seminary. I am in touch with friends who continue to work with Servants to Asia's Urban Poor, seeking to bring hope and blessing to a number of slum communities in this amazing city with its extreme contrasts.

Being here provides a good setting to begin to probe one of life and faith's difficult questions: 'How much change for the good may we expect in our world'?

The reason the Philippines provides a challenging setting in pursuing this basic question is because it, like so many other Third World countries, seems to experience so little change, despite significant aid and development strategies and despite the role of the church.

One seems to gain the impression that the way of the world simply continues. Despite the many signs of goodness

in every sphere of life, which call for celebration and
thankfulness, the old way and its problems persist. Poverty
continues. So do unjust work practices and inadequate
wages. So do corruption and cronyism. So does the reality
of an uneven playing field in the global economy and the
pain of foreign debt servicing. The story of pain seems to
go on and on, not only at the national level, but also at the
personal.

It is against this backdrop that I would like to speak
with you about the Reign, or Kingdom, of God. In particular
I would like to explore how this language may or may not
be helpful given the above scenario—that so little change
for the good seems to be happening in our world, and in
particular in the Third World.

What makes this discussion all the more difficult and
challenging is that the Reign of God does not seem to be
immediately accessible and evident in our world. Powerful
nations are in view. The power of large corporations
is evident. The influence of the media is well-known.
There are famous and influential persons. But how is the
Kingdom or Reign of God evident? How can we know it or
see it? And if it can be known, is it really all that significant
and powerful?

the kingdom of god and the church

There have been periods in the church's long two
thousand year history where it has been a powerful
institution. Popes were as powerful as Kings. It would have
been rather easy during those times to have said, 'Yes, I
can see the Kingdom of God. I can see it in the power
and influence of the leaders of the church. I can see it in
the magnificence of the cathedrals. I see it in the way the
church is influencing politics, education, the sciences and
the arts'.

It should, therefore, come as no surprise that the idea of the Kingdom of God became synonymous with the power of the church. The theology of the Kingdom was reduced to ecclesiology.

But there are obvious problems with this kind of vision. Can we simply reduce the presence of God and the purposes and power of God to what the church is and does? The answer to this would have to be a clear, 'NO'!

There are many reasons for such an answer. First, God is always greater and different than who we are and what we do. We are at best a poor reflection of God's ways, and the Christian witness in the world is first and foremost not a self-witness. The church does not point to itself in terms of its power, faithfulness and goodness. Instead, it points to God's love, grace and forgiveness.

Secondly, the church is always less than what it is called to be. While it is called to be the faithful servant of the Kingdom of God, the church stumbles in its belief and praxis. Even when the church was such a powerful institution it did not always use its power well. Instead, it became at times oppressive and self-serving.

In the modern world the church has also been less than what it was meant to be. The way the church in Germany largely embraced Nazi ideology is but one indication of the way the church has failed to be a sign of the Kingdom of God. Instead it embraced an idolatrous political ideology that was morally bankrupt. To equate the Reign of God with the church is to emasculate the nature of the Kingdom of God, and this gives power and status to the church which it should never receive.

The Kingdom of God instead is all about the nature of God as creator and redeemer extending 'his' love, care and goodness to all creation. The church is too small a vessel to contain all of this beneficence. Moreover, it is never the *source* of this goodness—only God is. So the church at most is but a sign, servant and sacrament of the Reign of God. The Reign of God is always far greater than the church.

All of this, of course, is not to suggest that the Kingdom of God has *nothing* to do with the church. I am only saying the two cannot be equated. What should be said is that the church is only truly church to the degree that it conforms itself to the Reign of God. What that looks like I will come to a little later in this letter.

the kingdom of god and the inner life

Those who embrace the more mystical traditions within Christianity have never been enamoured with the idea that the Reign of God can be expressed in terms of the power of the church. For them, the Kingdom of God is *only* an inner mystical reality experienced by people who have embraced the love of God in Christ Jesus and who live a life of inner piety through the Holy Spirit. Thus whether the church is doing poorly or well, the Kingdom of God is not primarily to be found there. It is to be found only in the inner life of individuals.

The appeal for this perspective is found in Jesus' exclamation, 'The Kingdom of God is within you' (Luke 17:21) and his further assertion before Pilate, 'My Kingdom is not of this world' (John 18:36).

Unlike the previous perspective, where the Reign of God is most visible in particular ways, in this vision the Kingdom of God is invisible. It lies hidden in the hearts and minds of people and in their personal practices of prayer and piety. The Reign of God is thus a religious psychological form of inwardness. It is personal and mysterious.

Clearly there is something valid in this vision of the Kingdom of God. The presence of God through the Holy Spirit at work in the heart and lives of individuals is part of the manifestation of the Kingdom. But it's not the whole mosaic. And the extent to which this is so will soon become clear.

the reign of god and utopia

There has always been a propensity on the part of individuals in renewal movements to believe that they are the last and fullest manifestation of the Kingdom of God and that the end of the world is at hand.

To some extent this perspective is close to the first vision with its identification of Kingdom and church. Only in this case, it is not the identification of traditional church and the Kingdom but the renewed church and the Kingdom. And the implication of this perspective is that the Reign of God is now most fully revealed in this renewal movement. This is where it is all at!

Now I need to point out that not all renewal movements are utopian. Many renewal movements spring up when there is a revitalization of personal faith and piety and the church is more vibrant in its worship, teaching, discipleship and service. Thus we have had renewal movements such as the Montanists in the early centuries of Christianity, the Waldensians in the Middle Ages, the Wesleyan renewal in eighteenth-century England and the charismatic renewal movement in the 1960s. There are, of course, many others.

But some are utopian. The central idea in these movements is that heaven comes to earth; here and now the fullness of life with God is possible and a whole new social order can come into being.[1] The Russian Leo Tolstoy held such ideas,[2] and the nineteenth century Oneida Society in the USA practised a religious utopianism.[3]

While it is very understandable that a group of people can envisage a perfect world within history, this is ultimately marked by idealism and escapism. The persistent worldliness of the world, the on-going reality of evil and the lack of justice in our divided world can hardly be denied.

Utopian movements always become perfectionistic and legalistic. They soon become cultish in orientation. And instead of reflecting the wideness of God's mercy and grace in a wounded world they become judgemental and are soon irrelevant.

the reign of god and eschatology

One of the ways that Christians have thought about the Kingdom of God has been to cast it wholly into the future. The present is not the time of the Kingdom. It is the church age. It is that period where Christians touched by the grace of God live in anticipation of the full coming of the Reign of God.

Thus the Kingdom is not substantially present. It lies in the long-awaited future. As a result, little can be seen now, and little can be expected. We are in an interim zone where the promise of the Kingdom awaits its fulfilment, and we live with the surety of what will come in the future with only present scraps from God's banqueting table. This becomes an attractive idea particularly when the church in the Western World is not doing well. While the utopian idea says that all can be well now, the eschatological vision says that all will be well in the future.

Now it is true that in the future God's reign will fully be revealed. But God is also with us now. God's grace is for this life. God's healing presence is with us here. And the good continues to sprout even in the asphalt of our social existence.

Future, yes! But present also, even though this presence is not the fullness of what will yet come.[4]

a biblical vision of the kingdom of god

The themes regarding the Reign of God—apart from the utopian version—belong together to form a mosaic. But these theological ideas don't give us a concrete enough picture regarding the Kingdom. To gain that we must turn to the biblical story.

In the Old Testament there is an emphasis on God's Kingship over Israel. But there is also a recognition that Yahweh's rule is over all. 'The Lord has established his throne in heaven and his Kingdom rules over all' (Psalm 103:19). This rulership is redemptive. God reigns in order to bless, to renew, to make whole and to uplift the poor and bring forth justice.

In the New Testament we note that the Kingdom of God remains an enduring theme. It is central to the preaching Jesus. '"The time has come", he said. "The Kingdom of God is near. Repent and believe the good news!"' (Mark 1:15). It is key to the mission of the disciples. 'He sent them out to preach the Kingdom of God and to heal the sick' (Luke 9:2). It is the focus of Jesus's post-resurrection appearances. 'He appeared to them over a period of forty days and spoke about the Kingdom of God' (Acts 1:3b). It is at the heart of Paul's preaching. 'Boldly and without hindrance he preached the Kingdom of God and taught about the Lord Jesus Christ' (Acts 28:31).

And finally, the Kingdom of God and its full manifestation is central to God's final future. 'The Kingdom of the World has become the Kingdom of our Lord and of his Christ and he will reign for ever and ever' (Revelation 11:15).

So what happens when the Kingdom of God draws near and breaks into our lives and our world? What are the signs that mark its coming? What is its melody? What sort of goodness does it bring?

Central to any manifestation of the Kingdom of God is an experience of the love of God and the forgiveness of sins (John 3:3, Mark 1:15, Luke 5:20). Linked to this is the healing power and presence of God and the banishment from our lives of the forces of darkness and oppression (Luke 7:18–23, Luke 11:20). Thus wherever and whenever the Kingdom of God comes to us there is the joy of salvation, the grace of forgiveness, the wholeness of God's healing presence and the manifestation of God's liberating work in pushing back the forces of darkness.

The One who brings this home to us is the go-between God, the Holy Spirit. The Spirit takes the blessings of Christ and flings them into our lives and world. Thus one of the signs of the in-breaking of the Reign of God is the presence and power of the Holy Spirit (Luke 24:49, John 14:15–17, Acts 1:8). When the Spirit comes there is an exposure of sin, there are healing gifts, there is abundant joy and the rigid and dry places are renewed with the showers of God's goodness (John 16:5, 11; 1 Corinthians 12:9, Isaiah 61:1–3).

The presence of the Kingdom of God is evident when reconciliation occurs, when communities of faith come into being or are renewed, when unity finds a common expression, when brotherhood and sisterhood, in the bonds of love and in common service, forms and grows. The Reign of God, while embedded in the life of the individual person, comes to expression in the *people* of God as a worshipping, teaching, sacramental, fellowshipping and serving community of faith (Luke 8:1–3, Galatians 3:26–28, Ephesians 2:14–22).

One of the signs of the Kingdom of God is when the love of God is translated into the love of neighbour in such a significant way that the poor and the enemy become the recipients of care and forgiveness. When God's care for the poor becomes our concern for the poor then the Kingdom of God is breaking in amongst us (Proverbs, 22:9, Isaiah 58:7, Luke 4:18-19, Matthew 26:34-40).[5]

In many parables Jesus speaks about the nature of the Kingdom of God. And besides its mystery and its growth, he refers to its subversive nature. Things are turned around. Things are turned the right side up: the poor are blessed and the meek inherit the earth.

The parables of reversal reflect this subversive activity of the Reign of God. The small, the stranger, the outsider—those we normally ignore or reject—become the models of the ethics of the Kingdom of God. A Samaritan becomes the bearer of the love of God (Luke 10:25-37) and a child a sign of the working of God (Matthew 18:1-6).

Mary's Song, or the Magnificant, most clearly expresses the ethics of reversal:

> He has shown strength with his arm; he has scattered the proud in the thoughts of their hearts. He has brought down the powerful from their thrones and lifted up the lowly; He has filled the hungry with good things and sent the rich away empty. (Luke 1:51–52, NRSV)

The Reign of God comes to us when the poor are seen as recipients of God's love and we respond in serving the poor and washing the feet of the world. This love for the poor involved Jesus in boundary breaking behaviour. Not only did Jesus reject current practices regarding Sabbath laws and not only did Jesus elevate the role of women, but Jesus invited all sorts of cultural outsiders including the poor, to his banqueting table (Luke 8:1–3, Luke 19:1–10, Matthew 22:1–4).[6]

a reflection

From the above it should be clear that the coming of the Kingdom of God amongst us does not look the same as someone having political or economic power. The Reign of God is not the same as the power a political party wields, even when that party claims to be essentially Christian. Nor is the Kingdom of God the same as the political, social and moral influence of the church. Moreover, the Kingdom of God is not something *we* build. Our activities of social justice in our broken world do not equate to a full manifestation of the Kingdom.

The Kingdom of God is the rule, blessing and beneficence of the Master of the Universe. It is the fruit of God's creative and redemptive activity. It is what God does in 'his' sustaining and healing activity. It is God's mending all of creation. The Kingdom of God is God's blessing and goodness spilling over into our lives, churches and our social institutions.

But what we do when *we* pray, share the good news, work for reconciliation, build communities of faith and do the work of justice can intersect and interface with God's Kingdom activity. A synchronicity can occur. God takes up the work of our hands and uses it for 'his' purposes. And what we do can be a reflection of the heart and purposes of God. But more often, God has to convert our actions into the grace and goodness that 'he' alone can bring forth. This perspective requires great humility on our part and a profound openness to the leading of the Holy Spirit.

So how much good then is possible in our world? Great good is possible, for God's heart is ever towards the world, seeking its transformation and healing. But we are not always humble servants of the King. We often build human religious kingdoms instead.[7] And the world has its own way of saying 'no' to the wisdom and grace of God.

My hope for you, Naasicaa, is that you will experience the grace of the Kingdom of God and seek to live as a sacrament of the Reign of God.

the galilean prophet and
the timeless christ

letter fifteen

As you know, Naasicaa, we are living in the eastside of the
city of Vancouver. We are happy to live in this interesting
neighbourhood. It is very multi-ethnic and we have Italians,
Greeks, Portuguese, Asians as well as First Nations people
living in this part of the city.

We are part of a church, Grandview Calvary Baptist
Church, which seeks to serve this neighbourhood. We
deliberately moved into this area to be part of this church
because it seeks to be an incarnational presence of Christ
to the people that live here, including many who are poor,
have disabilities or are political refugee claimants.

If you asked me, 'Why do you do this?' I would answer,
'Because of Christ'. But this of course needs further
explanation.

The cold January weather has brought a dumping
of snow, transforming the neighbourhood into a white

fairyland. I am thankful for our warm and snug basement apartment. It is from there that I am penning this letter.

the early witnesses

My main reason for starting my letter about Christ in this way is to highlight that for me and for millions of others, Christ is a present living reality rather than someone who only lived some two thousand years ago.

That a person called Jesus of Nazareth lived so long ago is beyond reasonable doubt. Not only do the writings called the gospels of the early church attest to this person, but Jewish and Roman authors of that time, who were more than skeptical about this Christ, also make reference to him.[1]

The challenge for us is not so much his historical existence, but the nature of who he was and is, and what he came to do. And for this we can only turn to the sources of early Christianity. In other words, we are invited to accept the testimony of the early followers of Jesus. Thus we are presented with an insiders' perspective, and we are asked to believe what they have to tell us about this person from Galilee.

The immediate concern that this brings is whether this prejudices their testimony. Can we trust the witness of persons who are already committed and who believe that Jesus is the Messiah, God's answer for a wayward humanity?

I think such a testimony is reasonable. No person who shares a testimony is neutral. But just as the words of commendation by a spouse about her husband are worth listening to, so the witness of Christ's followers is worth a careful hearing. This is particularly the case since their witness was in the public arena and in the midst of enemies and skeptics. Moreover, the witness of the early church was to people who had seen Jesus, heard him speak and had seen him crucified as an agitator with supposed subversive intent.

The witness of the early Christians is well summarized in Peter's public speech:

> Men of Israel, listen to this: Jesus of Nazareth was a man accredited by God to you by miracles, wonders, and signs, which God did among you through him, as you yourselves know. This man was handed over to you by God's set purposes and foreknowledge; and you, with the help of wicked men, put him to death by nailing him to the cross. But God raised him from the dead . . .
> (Acts 2:22–24a).

The hearers are then invited to believe that Jesus is the promised Messiah and the Saviour of the world. They are invited to believe this message and to 'repent and be baptized, every one of you, in the name of Jesus Christ for the forgiveness of your sins. And you will receive the gift of the Holy Spirit' (Acts 2:38).

In the light of the life he lived, the words he spoke, the healings he performed and his resurrection, Jesus was seen as more than a miracle worker and prophet. He was worshipped as Son of God, as God made manifest. This is clearly expressed by the Apostle Paul: 'in Christ God was reconciling the world to himself' (2 Corinthians 5:19a).

All of the writings of the New Testament are testimonials. They speak of God's saving and healing activity in Christ as well as the call to faith in Christ expressed in a life of worship, prayer and obedience. They speak of participation in the community of faith and a life of service in the world.

the many witnesses

Early Christianity began as a renewal movement within Judaism and developed its own ethos as a separate movement. It remained a marginal religious movement in the Roman Empire for the first several hundred years of its existence.

It was both tolerated and persecuted during these decades. But while vibrant in its beliefs it remained an absolute minority grouping. Scholars estimate that in the second century, with a population of some forty million in the Roman Empire, there were only some 200,000 Christians. This later changed when the Emperor Constantine converted to Christianity and it became the majority religion of the Empire.

There are many witnesses in the story of the church in history. Part of this remarkable story is the way Christianity moved onto foreign soil: from Palestine to Rome, to Persia, to India, to China, to barbaric Europe from 600 to 1000 A.D., to the Americas in the 1500s and from the 1800s on from the West to the rest of the world, leading to the present dominance of global Christianity in the Two-Thirds World. Some seventy percent of Christians live in the majority, i.e. the non-Western, world.

This story, Naasicaa, as I have written to you earlier, is a mixed story. There were times when the church was an exemplary witness to God's good news in Christ. At other times the church's witness was shameless, as in many of the Crusades from the years 1000 A.D. to the 1200s.

In this very long march of the church in history there are many witnesses whose faith and lives have passed into historical oblivion. But the witness of others has endured right up to the present, and you can read their writings: St. Augustine, St. Francis, Martin Luther, John Calvin, Teresa of Avila and John Wesley, just to mention a few. And there are many contemporary witnesses to encourage us to live the life of Christ with fidelity: Dietrich Bonhoeffer, Desmond Tutu, Mother Teresa, C.S. Lewis and Thomas Merton.

The testimony of many witnesses is important. This shows us how very different women and men, in different times and places, and in different groupings and traditions within the global Christian church, have sought to follow Christ and bring his goodness into the world.

my witness

I am happy to talk about my experience of Jesus, the Christ. Mine is but a little witness. And that is true for so many people who live 'ordinary' lives as spouses or singles, clergy or laity, artists or economists. And within the framework of family and friendships and work and play, they live out the love and vision of Jesus.

One's relationship with Jesus, mine included, is multi-textured. It is not one-dimensional, such as an intellectual orientation only. It is existential, intellectual, spiritual, communal and missional. And these dimensions are not stages but are part of the one picture.

By existential, I mean an encounter with Christ that touches the core of who one is and reorients one's life. This is a faith experience. It is also called conversion. In many ways this is a mystical experience. It is becoming aware of who Christ is and responding to Christ's presence so that Christ becomes experientially close.

I experienced this as a seventeen-year-old while going through an identity crisis accompanied by a deep search for an awareness of God. The words of John's Gospel, 'But to all who received him [Jesus], who believed in his name, he gave power to become children of God, who were born, not of blood or of the will of the flesh or of the will of man, but of

God' (John 1:12–13), came home to me like a shaft of light and a loving invitation.

While I have had my ups and downs in the spiritual life, including several experiences of the dark night of the soul, where God seemed very absent, this initial encounter with Christ, who came to save me and make me whole, has been the foundational impulse of my life.

One's relationship with Christ also has an intellectual orientation. What I mean by this is that one's faith in Christ seeks understanding. We are invited to be reflective regarding our relationship with Christ. This involves engaging the various witnesses of scripture and the long tradition of the church.

One's existential encounter with Christ cannot be a mere emotional experience. It needs to have a confessional shape. The witnesses of the biblical story do this. They experience and testify, and this testimony has an intellectual dimension. Listen to St Paul: 'It is Christ who lives in me. And the life I now live in the flesh I live by faith in the Son of God who loved me and gave himself for me' (Galatians 2:20b, NRSV). And the further testimony: 'He is the image of the invisible God, the first born of all creation . . . in him all things hold together' (Colossians 1:15–17, NRSV).

The main reason why I completed seminary training was not so much to become a clergy person. It had to do with a desire to grow in my understanding of the Christian faith. Thus theology is important. We are invited to love God with all of our mind, not simply with our heart.

The intellectual dimensions of one's faith also involve thinking about the implications of one's faith for one's involvement in society. But I will say something about that under the missional dimension.

The Christian faith and life is a particular form of spirituality. And at its very heart this has to do with the Spirit. Christ is present with us through the Spirit. Not only 'were we all made to drink of one Spirit' but 'to each is given the manifestation of the Spirit for the common good' (1 Corinthians 12:13b and 7, NRSV).

Thus living the Christian life involves a Christo-mysticism where Christ is made real and present to us by the Holy Spirit, and this Spirit shapes us into a Christ conformity so that we manifest the fruits of love, joy and peace and the gifts of healing and prophecy, among other gifts and graces. I experience my relationship with Christ not in terms of self-effort, but more as gift and blessing. The Spirit sustains and empowers me in this.

While the experience of Christ is personal, it is also communal. Christ is not simply my personal treasured possession. It is more the other way round. I am his. And in belonging to him, I also belong to all the others whom he has graced and called. And through Christ I belong to humanity as a witness and servant of Christ. Thus I am part of the community of faith because Christ has called diverse women and men together to share a common life of worship, teaching, sacrament, fellowship and service.

This, as I have pointed out in another letter, is a big challenge for us today. Marked by Western individualism and a consumer mentality we find it difficult to live the communal aspects of our faith. But the testimony of the early church is clear: 'We are all baptized by one Spirit into one body' (1 Corinthians 12:13a).[2]

What this means is that I experience the presence of Christ both in my personal reflections and prayers and also in my joining with others in the common journey of faith. It also means that in joining hands, the community of faith can be involved in communal witness, care for others and the work of justice.

This is what I mean by the missional dimension of the Christian life. Christ's blessings are for all. Yet not all are predisposed towards Christ. Some find him irrelevant.

Others don't care. Thus as both the gathered church and as
the scattered church we are called to be little lights of the
Great Light, Jesus Christ.

the sign of his presence

Naasicaa, Christ comes to us at both the regular
and traumatic intersections of our life. His is a seeking
presence. Sometimes he comes in the full light of his power
and love. Sometimes he comes in disguise in the forgotten
and vulnerable ones in our society.

The signs of his presence are everywhere: the comfort
of a stranger, the goodness of a teacher, the blessing of
a parent, the prayer of the unknown, the challenge of a
friend, the grace of the sacrament, the silence of the seeking
heart. 'Come, all you who are thirsty . . . Seek the Lord
while he may be found . . .' (Isaiah 55:1a and 6a).

The snow is falling again, ever so softly, ever so gently.
It covers all and wraps everything up in virginal purity. So
it is with the Spirit of Christ: falling upon us, ever so gently,
bringing us new life.

time, finitude, death and the power of hope and transcendence

letter sixteen

While I am not preoccupied with the subject of death, I do think quite a bit about it. I hope this does not mean that I am morbid.

I was born in the midst of World War II, so from that fact alone, it is not surprising that death has been close to home for me. And as a young man working in several Aboriginal communities in Western Australia, death was all around me—not only the cultural 'death' of a people, but also physical death due to a very high infant mortality rate. And death of grandparents and parents are part of this textured story.

As a young boy growing up in Holland, my first concrete encounter with death was the serious illness of my grandmother. My father broke the news to me that she was sick and needed my prayers. I refused to pray and soon afterwards she died. For years I felt to blame for her death. I have also felt guilty about working overseas while my parents were aging; I was not there for them, not even in the weeks and days before they passed away.

I am quite sure, Naasicaa, that you must be wondering where this is going and why I am writing to you about this. When one is young one tends not to think about time, finitude and death. Moreover, our contemporary culture is in a state of avoidance regarding these matters. Ours is a culture that venerates youth and beauty. But the faith traditions do deal with these subjects, particularly as they explore the power of hope in the face of tragedy and death.[1]

keeping time

Like all of us you are aware of chronological time. You possibly also complain that there is not enough time, particularly when you are out with friends and having a good time. The fact that we speak of having a good time also means that there are other forms of time. When time creeps along. When we are bored. When we have to do things we don't enjoy and time seems to drag endlessly by.

Thus while chronological time ticks regularly along, our experience of time varies significantly. Kissing and having a cuddle with one's boyfriend can turn seeming minutes into an hour. In a similar way, artists, musicians and writers can lose all sense of time. So can daydreamers.

In practicing the disciplines of the spiritual life it is also possible to have a very different sense of time. Worship, prayer, the practice of solitude and meditation may all be experienced more as a 'timeless' now rather than as ordinary chronological time.

What makes the topic of time even more fascinating is the sense we have that 'now is the time' to do something. The Greeks knew this as *Kairos*. Whether this sense of time comes through rational calculation, intuition, divine guidance or through circumstances coming together, it matters little. We have a hunch, sometimes a strong belief, that *now* is the time to go somewhere or to make a certain commitment. We know that we have to seize the day!

Thus there is such a thing as auspicious time. This time is all about timing. We sense that now is the *right* time. This has many ramifications. We talk of a good time to visit, the right time to make an apology, an opportune time to start a new business venture.

Much less exciting is the idea of wasted time. We go and do something or visit someone with certain expectations and come away disappointed. It all turned out differently than we had expected. It was somehow unproductive. Thus wasted time is lost time, we think.

The above comments suggest that our experience of time is rather complex. And possibly the greatest complexity is that we hold together in our very being both a sense of the past, the experience of the present and our leaning into and anticipation of the future.

the past

Our personal past is important. It has shaped us. Both the good and the bad have been the anvil on which our lives have been forged. For the good we are invited to be thankful. For the bad we are called to be forgiving. But the bad, while it may have wounded us, has also shaped us. Much of life is both overcoming and compensating for what has pushed us down and hurt us. This does not mean that we should dwell on the past or make endless archaeological expeditions into our inner being. But awareness of our past rather than its denial is important for our growth and wellness.

From a spiritual point of view it is important to see the signs of God's care in our past. The ultimate expression of this is God's shaping hand at the very genesis of our being. The psalmist exclaims, 'My frame was not hidden from you when I was made in the secret place' (Psalm 139:15a).

The depth of the presence of God in our past is evidenced by its reality when we were not even looking, when we were not aware. Hosea the prophet knows something about this. 'When Israel was a child I loved him and out of Egypt I called my son. But the more I called Israel the further they went from me' (Hosea 11:1–2a).

Far better that the opposite occurs, that our past is marked by the appreciated and celebrated presence of God and 'his' goodness. Better that we can confess with the psalmist, 'Surely goodness and mercy shall follow me all the days of my life' (Psalm 23:6a, NRSV).

While both our personal history and the general ethos of our time shape us, we are not wholly bound by these. Our past can be reframed or reconfigured. Or to use religious language, it can be redeemed. What I mean by this is that from the place of distance and greater maturity and through the gentle gift of forgiveness, we can come to the place where we make better sense of the folly and brokenness of our past.

But the process of reappropriating our past with the oil of healing is not the only way that we break free. It is also our anticipation of an envisaged future that reshapes us.

facing the future

As human beings we lean into the future. We have plans, hopes and dreams. We see possibilities of what we may do and become. While some of this may be mere wishful thinking and will soon evaporate under the blighted sun of realism, not all dreams come to nothing. In fact the opposite may occur. We can begin to live our dreams in the now and lay a tenuous foundation for their future realization. Future hopes become particularly potent if we have a sense that this is the direction for our lives or that God is leading us in this direction.

finitude

It usually does not take a person too long to realize that we human beings live our lives within a certain boundedness. We experience that we are never wholly free nor always full of energy. The rhythms of life—of activity and rest, work and sleep, eating and playing, thinking and doing—express this boundedness. We also soon realize that we live with all sorts of limitations. We are not in every way beautiful or handsome, not always smart and not always wise. Nor are we as powerful as we might wish to be. This invites us to embrace our finiteness and our vulnerabilities.

The psalmist knows something about this blatant realism. He confesses, 'For all our days pass away under your wrath; our years come to an end like a sigh. The days of our life are seventy years, or perhaps eighty, if we are strong; even then their span is only toil and trouble; they are soon gone and we fly away' (Psalm 90:9–10, NRSV).

But why should I think about this, you may well ask? My response is most basic: we need to embrace our finiteness lest we live our lives with an unhealthy striving that catapults us into the sphere of the gods, but which has us crashing to the ground when we least expect it.

Let me first come at this existentially and later theologically. Between an unfortunate passivism and an unhealthy egoism lies an intermediate zone of human action and endeavour that celebrates our giftedness and accepts our limitations. In this zone, one can work hard and strive to achieve certain goals, create beauty, produce certain goods and do some of the myriad of things we human beings busy ourselves with. But our activism is consistent with our being, so that we are not doing violence to ourselves by radically over-extending ourselves and working outside the sphere of our giftedness. Put most simply, we are not trying to be other or more than what we are.

When we look at professionals who are burnt out and many workers who are experiencing stress-related illnesses, then we realize that this is no trifling matter. Our life depends on embracing a sanity about who we are and what we do.

Theologically our propensity to seeking to become more than what we are is explained by our loss of the perfection of the Edenic garden and our non-arrival in God's final future. In between these two visions we long for perfection and completion. To put all of this much more particularly, the original temptation was, 'You will be like God' (Genesis 3:5b). And humanity's restless striving is evidenced by the quest for greatness and power. This has led to endless forms of demagoguery.

I would like to propose, Naasicaa, that the embrace of our finiteness and limitation is a great blessing. It is a grace because it rightly situates us. We are not God. We are creatures of worth, dignity and creativity. But we are also limited and less than perfect. We make mistakes and do wrong. We can also do much good.

So rather than soaring to be among the gods—which are usually the gods of our own making anyway—we are called instead to inhabit more deeply our own being. We can become 'at home' in our own skin. And we can then rightly acknowledge God for who God is and become 'godlike' through God's transforming and healing presence rather than through our own efforts.

death

The marks of death are already inscripted on our fragile hands at the moment of birth. Death is a given in the journey of life.

And death, when it comes, is something we need to face rather than scramble to avoid. This of course is not to suggest that we should not resist the forces of death through good health practices, the use of medicine and availing ourselves of spiritual healing ministries.

I have already spoken to you, Naasicaa, of many forms of 'death'. We can speak of leaving as a 'little dying'. Relinquishment is a form of death. So is a spiritual surrender to the will and purposes of God. But here I am speaking about the end of our life.

Is there hope in death? Is there life beyond death? While many people see death as the end, Christianity holds before us the hope of the resurrection and a new life in the world to come. The Apostle Paul puts this most clearly:

> So will it be with the resurrection of the dead.
> The body that is sown is perishable, it is raised
> imperishable; it is sown in dishonour, it is raised
> in glory; it is sown in weakness, it is raised in
> power; it is sown a natural body, it is raised a
> spiritual body (1 Corinthians 15:42–44).

So what about that, one may well ask? Death is far away. And once I am gone, I am gone. Does belief in an afterlife have any importance?

I would like to propose a strong 'yes', for a variety of reasons. But my 'yes' has nothing to do with a form of escapism in which one says, 'Never mind about this life, there is a better life to come'. This leads to a world-denying form of Christianity and leaves one passive in our world.

I would like to reorient the phrase to read as follows: because there is a life to come, we can live this life in faith, with risk-taking and with prophetic radicality. To put that differently, because in Christianity there is a vision for the healing of all things, the resurrection and the expectation of new heavens and a new earth, I can live my life differently in the here and now.

Let me suggest some perspectives. The first is that the hope in the life to come means that what happens here is *never* the last word. God has the last word and 'his' is the final future. This relativises our ideologies and our projects. The human word, the human project is never the ultimate perspective. And historically we have seen again and again how political systems and social ideologies have claimed an ultimacy and have become idolatrous.

Secondly, hope in the resurrection and faith in the life to come mean that what I do and become is not the ultimate meaning of my existence. If this was the case I would surely be disappointed. Many great people have lived messy lives. And famous people and world leaders have become quite disillusioned with their own achievements.

The idea that God loves me for who I am rather than for what I achieve is a liberating concept. And it is a blessing, indeed, that my future lies not in what I have done or become but in God's new future of a transformed self in a new 'world'!

Thirdly, the challenge in living the Christian life is to anticipate this final future. We won't ever do this fully. But God's final healing of all things can find expression now in the healing of our lives and communities. God's Kingdom of *shalom* means that we can work for peace now in our families, communities and the wider society.

a personal reflection

I am back in Brisbane. It's hot. And the sky is sultry. It is full of the promise of much needed rain.

I will soon be in a major transition again: leaving Canada in order to give more attention to working in Asia. Leaving is a form of 'death'. I do transitions with difficulty and always feel torn.

This to some extent is a small foreshadowing of the great tearing that will take place: torn from family and friends and torn from this life. This is always an act of violence. But in being torn asunder lies the gift of new life.

Paul knew this well. He writes, 'Do you know that all of us who have been baptized into Christ Jesus were baptized into his death? Therefore we have been buried with him by baptism into death, so that, just as Christ was raised from the dead by the glory of the Father, so we too might walk in newness of life' (Romans 6:3–4, NRSV).

afterword

letter seventeen

I have enjoyed writing these letters to you, Naasicaa. I had first thought that I would be able to write them fairly quickly. But this has not been the case. It has stretched out over several years. As a result of this drawn out process I have had to go back and reread my letters to you. And while I am generally happy with what I have written, I am a little bit disappointed as well.

There are things that I have not touched on. If it is true that faith has implications for all of one's life then everything needs to be thought about. I have not covered everything—this is impossible—but I do wonder whether I have missed some of your more pressing issues and concerns.

What also worries me is whether I have been courageous enough in tackling various issues or whether I have simply re-stated more traditional religious positions. This could reflect that I am much older and have settled for a more traditional religious faith and set of perspectives regarding the world. So even though I have tended to regard myself as a more 'radical' Christian I may be fooling myself.

My greater sense of disappointment, however, lies elsewhere. I don't think that I have been able to tell the story of faith with the winsomeness and joy that it deserves. I often feel stuck for words. Within my own being I sense the beauty of God's presence and see the world with eyes of faith and hope. But I can't bring this sense of wonder and enchantment under words. And maybe I am not emotional enough as well. My more austere Reformed upbringing does not help in finding the language of ecstasy.[1]

So at best these letters are but a meager offering. And maybe that is all that one can do. The mystery of God is beyond us. The life of faith, like a floating iceberg, remains partly hidden even from ourselves. The way that God works in the world through and apart from the community of faith is also always the way of surprise.

This afterword therefore cannot redeem what I have failed to do in my letters. But I do wish to say a few things by way of closure.

I have no way of knowing what will unfold in our world regarding the search for faith and spirituality. What is clear is that secularity does not eliminate the human quest for spiritual meaning and transcendence. Neither the secularity of state communism in the former Soviet Union and the present China, nor the secularity of capitalism have answered the human desire for ultimate meaning rooted in faith and love.

What is also clear is that the collapse of Christendom in the Western World and the present serious credibility challenges facing the church are not the end of the story. The church has previously experienced various 'dark ages' and is re-experiencing one now. It will again, I am sure, rise like a phoenix out of its own ashes. This renewal is never automatic but rather has everything to do with God's renewing and revitalizing Spirit. The part we are called to play is one of faith, humility, prayer and service.

So in closing and in wishing you well as you ponder these letters, let me again state the heart of the matter of the matters of the heart.

I believe that we cannot live well simply within the ethos of a rationalistic and scientific worldview. Yes, these perspectives have their place as we seek to explain things and make things work. But we are also creatures who hope, love and dream. We may be rational, but we are also intuitive. We may be scientific, but we are also artistic and imaginative. Therefore, I think we may safely say that spirituality is as much a part of who we are as is our physicality. We not only have a body, we also have an inner life.

In these letters I have sought to talk about Christian spirituality. I believe that while there may be disinterest in the West regarding this form of spirituality, unlike the great interest in the Majority World, there are great riches that may be re-discovered there. The most central idea in this spirituality is that a loving and healing God seeks us out in Christ through the Spirit to renew us and make us whole. This is the good news of the gospel that 'God so loved the world that he gave his only Son, so that everyone who believes in him may not perish but may have eternal life' (John 3:16, NRSV).

The presence of Christ with us becomes the joyous comfort and centre out of which we live. The good news of the gospel and the whole biblical story becomes the framework for guiding our thinking and acting. The community of faith sustains us in the journey of following Christ's way. And whether one is a house spouse, farmer, carpenter, artist, economist or politician, one seeks to live and serve in such a way that the things we do are life-giving to others instead of death-dealing.

This way of living includes a special attentiveness to the vulnerable, the marginalized and the poor. This is also the way of Christ, as is the practice of peacemaking and the work of reconciliation.

The experience of the presence of Christ does not come by way of coercion or method. It comes by way of seeking and revelation, but more importantly, it comes because Christ is the seeking God.

notes

Letter One

1. See in particular the work of Hans-Georg Gadamer, especially his *Philosophical Hermeneutics* (Berkeley: University of California Press, 1976).

2. See Philip Jenkins, *The Next Christendom: The Coming of Global Christianity* (Oxford: Oxford University Press, 2002).

Letter Two

1. See N. Wolterstroff, *Until Justice and Peace Embrace* (Grand Rapids: Eerdmans, 1983).

2. See R. J. Bernstein, *Beyond Objectivism and Relativism* (Oxford: Basil Blackwell, 1983).

3. P. Berger & T. Luckmann, *The Social Construction of Reality* (New York: Doubleday, 1966).

Letter Three

1. See Martin Heidegger, *Being and Time* (London: SCM Press, 1962).

2. See Zygmunt Bauman, *Post-Modernity and its Discontents* (Cambridge: Polity Press, 1997).

3. See Eberhard Bethge, *Dietrich Bonhoeffer: A Biography* (Minneapolis: Fortress Press, 2000). See also my *Seize the Day with Dietrich Bonhoeffer* (Colorado Springs: Pinon Press, 2000).

4. See J. M. Washington, ed., *A Testament of Hope: The Essential Writings and Speeches of Martin Luther King, Jr.* (New York: Harper San Francisco, 1986). See also my *Let My People Go with Martin Luther King, Jr.* (Colorado Springs: Pinon Press, 2004).

5. See in particular Erik Erikson, *Childhood and Society* (New York: Norton, 1963).

6. See Max Weber, three volume *Economy and Society* (New York: Badminster Press, 1968).

7. See Jacques Ellul, *Hope in Time of Abandonment* (New York: The Seabury Press, 1973). See also my *Resist the Powers with Jacques Ellul* (Colorado Springs: Pinon Press, 2000).

Letter Four

1. See J. Grant-Thomson, *Jodie's Story* (Sydney: Anzea, 1991) for something of this story.

2. See Mende Nazer, *Slave* (London: Virago, 2004) as an example of contemporary slavery.

3. See R. Bellah, et. al., *Habits of the Heart* (Berkeley: University of California Press, 1984).

4. See E.A. & J.D. Whitehead, *Community of Faith: Crafting Christian Communities Today* (Mystic: Twenty-Third Publications, 1992).

5. See Martin Luther King, Jr., *Where Do We Go From Here: Chaos or Community?* (New York: Bantam, 1968).

6. For one person's downward mobility see Henri Nouwen, *The Road to Daybreak: A Spiritual Journey* (New York: Doubleday, 1988) and my *Dare to Journey With Henri Nouwen* (Colorado Springs: Pinon Press, 2000).

7. See Rollo May, *Power and Innocence: A Search for the Sources of Violence* (New York: Norton, 1974).

8. See Leonardo and Clodovis Boff, *Introducing Liberation Theology* (Maryknoll: Orbis, 1988) and my *Cry Freedom with Voices from the Third World* (Sydney: Albatross Books, 1998).

Letter Five

1. See my good colleague's work on this topic: R. Paul Stevens, *The Other Six Days* (Grand Rapids: Eerdmans, 2000).

2. See Lesslie Newbigin, *The Gospel in Pluralist Society* (Grand Rapids: Eerdmans, 1989).

3. See Thomas Kuhn, *The Structure of Scientific Revolutions* (Chicago: University of Chicago Press, 1962).

4. See the discussion on Feuerbach in Colin Brown, *Philosophy and the Christian Faith* (London: IVP, 1973).

5. Consult J. Hick & P. Knitter, eds., *The Myth of Christian Uniqueness* (London: SCM, 1987).

6. See Thomas Wolf's telling *The Bonfire of the Vanities* (New York: Bantam, 1988).

7. See T.R. Henn, *The Bible as Literature* (London: Lutterworth Press, 1970).

8. See J.S. Croatto, *Exodus: A Hermeneutics of Freedom* (Maryknoll: Orbis, 1981).

9. See my book *Life in Full Stride* (Vancouver: Regent College Publishing, 2004).

10. See Robert Banks, *God the Worker* (Sydney: Albatross Books, 1992).

11. See Sally McFague, *Metaphorical Theology* (Philadelphia: Fortress Press, 1982).

12. You may wish to read Colin Gunton, *The Promise of a Trinitarian Theology* (Edinburgh: T & T Clark, 1997).

13. See Athol Gill, *Life on the Road: The Gospel Basis for a Messianic Lifestyle* (Sydney: Lancer, 1989).

14. See her *One Heart Full of Love* (Ann Arbor: Servant Books, 1988). Also see my *Wash the Feet of the World with Mother Teresa* (Colorado Springs: Pinon Press, 2004).

15. See Donald Kraybill, *The Upside-Down Kingdom* (Scottdale: Herald Press, 1978).

16. You might like to read this amazing story in J.L. Gonzalez, *The Story of Christianity: The Early Church to the Present Day* (Peabody: Prince Press, 2004).

17. See Henri Nouwen, *Sabbatical Journey: The Diary of his Final Year* (New York: Crossroad, 1998) for a discussion of this kind of vulnerability.

Letter Six

1. See F. Copleston, *A History of Philosophy* (New York: Doubleday, 1985), vols. VII–IX. For a discussion on Hegel, see pp. 159–247.

2. See R.Bendix, *Max Weber: An Intellectual Portrait* (Garden City: Anchor Books, 1962), 49–79.

3. Søren Kierkegaard, *Either/Or, Vol. II* (Garden City: Anchor Books, 1959).

4. See Jacques Ellul, *The Technological Bluff* (Grand Rapids: Eerdmans, 1990).

5. See A.T. Hennelly, ed., *Liberation Theology: A Documentary History* (Maryknoll: Orbis, 1990).

6. One book that reflects something of that very varied movement is Arthur Blessitt, *Turned on to Jesus* (New York: Hawthorn Books, 1971).

7. See Thomas Merton, *New Seeds of Contemplation* (Norfolk: New Directions, 1961).

8. Here you may wish to read Thomas Merton, *Contemplation in a World of Action* (Garden City: Doubleday, 1971) and my *Seek the Silences with Thomas Merton* (London: SPCK, 2003).

9. For a helpful statement of theological themes within the Evangelical tradition, see Stanley Grenz, *Theology for the Community of God* (Grand Rapids: Eerdmans; Vancouver: Regent College Publishing, 2000).

10. Here the writings of St. John of the Cross may be helpful. See particularly his 'Dark Night of the Soul' in *The Complete Works of St. John of the Cross* (Westminster: The Newman Bookshop, 1946).

11. Karl Rahner *Theological Investigations* (London: Darton, Longman & Todd, 1971), 7:15.

12. See Malcolm Muggeridge, *Something Beautiful for God* (London: Collins, 1972) and Mother Teresa, *No Greater Love* (Novato: New World Library, 2002).

13. See Dietrich Bonhoeffer's classic, *Life Together* (London: SCM, 1954).

Letter Seven

1. See my *Catch the Wind* (Vancouver: Regent College Publishing, 2005).

2. See Darrell Guder, et. al., *Missional Church* (Grand Rapids: Eerdmans, 1998).

3. See Alan Jamieson, *A Churchless Faith* (Wellington: Philip Garside Publishing, 2000).

4. See Karl Rahner, *The Shape of the Church to Come* (London: SPCK, 1974).

5. See Emil Brunner, *The Misunderstanding of the Church* (London: Lutterworth, 1952).

6. See Edwin Judge, *The Social Pattern of Christian Groups in the First Century* (London: Tyndale Press, 1960).

7. See Bengt Holmberg, *Paul and Power* (Lund: CWK Gleerup, 1978).

8. See R. & J. Banks, *The Church Comes Home* (Sydney: Albatross Books, 1996) and L. Boff, *Ecclesiogenesis* (Maryknoll: Orbis, 1986).

9. Quoted in D. F. Durnbaugh, *The Believer's Church: The History and Character of Radical Protestantism* (London: Macmillan, 1970), 23.

10. See D. J. Gouwens, *Kierkegaard as Religious Thinker* (Cambridge: Cambridge University Press, 1996).

11. You might like to read the challenging small book by E. Arnold, *Why We Live in Community* (Farmington: Plough Publishing, 1995).

12. Dietrich Bonhoeffer, *Letters and Papers from Prison* (London: Collins, 1971).

13. Karl Barth, *Church Dogmatics: The Doctrine of Reconciliation* (Edinburgh: T & T Clark, 1962), IV/3, II.

14. N. Wolterstorff, *Until Justice and Peace Embrace* (Grand Rapids: Eerdmans, 1983).

15. Jacques Ellul, *The Presence of the Kingdom*, 2nd ed. (Colorado Springs: Helmers & Howard, 1989).

16. D. Kraybill, *The Upside-Down Kingdom* (Scottdale: Herald Press, 1978).

17. See my 'Lower the Drawbridge: Bring Social Justice Home', *Renewal Journal* 3 (1994), 3–9.

18. You may wish to read Thomas Merton, *The Monastic Journey* (London: Sheldon Press, 1977).

19. See also Jean Vanier, *From Brokenness to Community* (New York: Paulist, 1992).

20. John Drane, *The McDonaldization of the Church* (London: Darton, Longman & Todd, 2000).

21. To gain some sense of this regarding Latin America see G. Cook, ed., *The New Face of the Church in Latin America* (Maryknoll: Orbis, 1994). For Asia see S. Athyal, ed., *The Church in Asia Today* (Singapore: Asia Lausanne Committee for World Evangelization, 1996).

22. See D. W. Ferm, *Third World Liberation Theologies: A Reader* (Maryknoll: Orbis, 1986).

23. You may wish to read J. O'Halloran, *Small Christian Communities: A Pastoral Companion* (Maryknoll: Orbis, 1996).

24. See the little classic by Richard Foster, *Celebration of Discipline: The Path to Spiritual Growth* (London: Hodder and Stoughton, 1980).

25. Craig van Gelder, ed. *Confident Witness – Changing World* (Grand Rapids: Eerdmans, 1999).

26. A good read of the Bonhoeffer story is R. Wind, *Dietrich Bonhoeffer: A Spoke in the Wheel* (Grand Rapids: Eerdmans, 1992).

Letter Eight

1. See R. Paul Stevens, *The Other Six Days* (Grand Rapids: Eerdmans, 2000).

2. I touched on some of these themes in my book *Seek the Silences with Thomas Merton* (London: SPCK, 2003).

3. See L.S. Cunningham & K.J. Egan, *Christian Spirituality: Themes from the Tradition* (New York: Paulist Press, 1996).

4. For a brief discussion, see Diogenes Allen, *Spiritual Theology: The Theology of Yesterday for Spiritual Help Today* (Cambridge, MA: Cowley, 1997) 86–89.

5. For the general setting of early Christianity see S. Benko & J.T. O'Rouke, eds., *The Catacombs and the Colosseum: The Roman Empire as the Setting of Primitive Christianity* (Valley Forge: Judson Press, 1971).

6. See my *Whispers from the Edge of Eternity: Reflections on Life and Faith in a Precarious World* (Vancouver: Regent College Publishing, 2005), 113.

7. St. John of the Cross, *Dark Night of the Soul* (New York: Riverhead, 2002).

8. Rollo May, *Power and Innocence* (New York: Norton, 1974).

9. Fredrick Copleston, *A History of Philosophy* (New York: Doubleday, 1985), 7: 404.

10. See J. Moltmann, *The Crucified God* (Minneapolis: Fortress Press, 1993).

11. See Henri Nouwen, *Reaching Out: The Three Movements of the Spiritual Life* (New York: Doubleday, 1975).

12. See the wonderful little classic of Evelyn Underhill, *The Spiritual Life* (London: Hodder & Stoughton, 1937).

13. You may wish to read about the Desert Fathers. See Helen Waddell, trans., *The Desert Fathers* (New York: Vintage Books, 1998).

14. Thomas Merton, *Contemplative Prayer* (London: Darton, Longman & Todd, 1969).

15. S. Chan, *Pentecostal Theology and the Christian Spiritual Tradition* (Sheffield: Sheffield Academic Press, 2000).

16. See J.D. Faubion, *The Shadows and Lights of Waco* (Princeton: Princeton University Press, 2001).

17. M. Scott Peck, *People of the Lie* (London: Rider, 1983).

Letter Nine

1. G.E. Ganss, *Ignatius of Loyola: The Spiritual Exercises and Selected Works* (New York: Paulist Press, 1991).

2. H-G. Gadamer, *Heidegger's Ways* (Albany: State University of New York Press, 1994), 63.

3. D. Keirsey & M. Bates, *Please Understand Me: Character & Temperament Types* (Del Mar, CA: Prometheus Nemesis, 1984).

4. D.R. Riso, *Understanding the Enneagram* (Boston: Houghton Mifflin, 1990).

5. An interesting read is the theologian Paul Tillich, *The Courage to Be* (London: Collins, 1962). And a writer who was very helpful to me in younger days was the Swiss psychiatrist Paul Tounier. You would enjoy his *The Meaning of Persons* (London: SCM, 1957).

6. See my *Gadamer's Dialogical Hermeneutic* (Heidelberg Universitatsverlag: C. Winter, 1999), 44.

7. You may wish to read the interesting book by Janet Hagberg, *Real Power* (Minneapolis: Winston Press, 1984).

8. You may enjoy his *Letters to Malcolm: Chiefly on Prayer* (London: Fontana, 1964).

9. D. M. Thomas, *Alexander Solzhenitsyn: A Century in his Life* (New York: St Martin, Press, 1998).

10. Henri Nouwen, *With Open Hands* (Notre Dame: Ave Maria Press, 1972).

11. M. Scott Peck, *In Search of Stones* (New York: Hyperion, 1995).

Letter Ten

1. You may want to read A. Bloom, *The Closing of the American Mind* (New York: Simon & Schuster, 1987).

2. For two thoughtful books about living life with passion and commitment, see Dietrich Bonhoeffer, *The Cost of Discipleship* (London: SCM, 1959) and Donald Kraybill, *The Upside Down Kingdom* (Scottdale: Herald Press, 1978).

3. For something of the history of this see J. J. Suurmond, *Word and Spirit at Play* (Grand Rapids: Eerdmans, 1995).

4. A helpful book that sets out the prophetic vision of the Old Testament is Walter Brueggemann, *The Prophetic Imagination* (Minneapolis: Fortress Press, 1978).

5. Harry Blamires, *The Christian Mind* (Vancouver: Regent College Publishing, 2005).

6. The person who has written well about this is Segundo Galilea in his book *Following Jesus* (Maryknoll: Orbis, 1984). See my *Wash the Feet of the World With Mother Teresa* (Colorado Springs: Pinon Press, 2004).

Letter Eleven

1. One of the books that inspired us was Edith Schaeffer, *Hidden Art* (London: The Norfolk Press, 1971).

2. One of Jacques Ellul's helpful books is *The Presence of the Kingdom* (New York: Seabury, 1967).

3. You may want to check out Hans-Georg Gadamer, *Truth and Method* (New York: Seabury, 1975) about the power and possibility of questions.

Letter Twelve

1. See M. Kelsey, *Encounter with God* (Minneapolis: Bethany Fellowship, 1972), 110–117.

2. Letty Russell, ed., *Feminist Interpretation of the Bible* (Philadelphia: Westminster Press, 1985), 139.

3. L.S. Cunningham & K.J. Egan, *Christian Spirituality* (New York: Paulist Press, 1996), 123–142.

4. M. Battle, *Reconciliation: The Ubuntu Theology of Desmond Tutu* (Cleveland: Pilgrim Press, 1997).

5. P.D. Hanson, *The People Called* (San Francisco: Harper & Row, 1986).

6. G. Hancock, *Lords of Poverty* (New York: The Atlantic Monthly Press, 1989).

Letter Thirteen

1. See R. Banks, *All the Business of Life* (Sydney: Albatross Books, 1987).

2. See my *Resist the Powers with Jacques Ellul* (Colorado Springs: Pinon, 2000).

3. M.J. Dawn, *Keeping the Sabbath Wholly: Ceasing, Resting, Embracing, Feasting* (Grand Rapids: Eerdmans, 1989).

Letter Fourteen

1. See the classic by N. Cohn, *The Pursuit of the Millennium* (London: Paladin, 1970).

2. Leo Tolstoy, *The Kingdom of God is Within You* (New York: Noonday Press, 1961).

3. Bryan Wilson, *Religious Sects: A Sociological Study* (London: Weidenfeld & Nicolson, 1970), 181–184.

4. For the above themes and emphasis regarding the Kingdom of God, see H.A. Snyder, *Models of the Kingdom of God* (Nashville: Abingdon, 1991).

5. R. Kinsler & G. Kinsler, *The Biblical Jubilee and the Struggle for Life* (Maryknoll: Orbis, 1999).

6. A. Gill, *The Fringes of Freedom* (Sydney: Lancer, 1990).

7. See Jacques Ellul, *The Subversion of Christianity* (Grand Rapids: Eerdmans, 1986).

Letter Fifteen

1. N. Perrin, *The New Testament: An Introduction* (New York: Harcourt Brace Jovanovich, 1974), 283–284.

2. R. Banks, *Paul's Idea of Community* (Sydney: Anzea, 1979).

Letter Sixteen

1. J. Moltmann, *Theology of Hope* (Minneapolis: Fortress, 1993).

Letter Seventeen

1. See my *Seek the Silences with Thomas Merton* (London: SPCK, 2003).

www.ingramcontent.com/pod-product-compliance
Lightning Source LLC
Chambersburg PA
CBHW032054080426
42733CB00006B/272